TOO
SMALL
TO
WIN

How a small-town team beat all odds in
one of the greatest underdog stories
in the history of sports

COACH RON MARTIN & RANDY LOWE

Published by Caldwell 6 Pack, LLC

ISBN - 979-8-9922332-2-3

CONTENTS

FOREWORD

You are about to learn how a small-town team of boys from a tiny high school in an impoverished southeastern Ohio community rose to seemingly impossible heights. Together, against all odds, they won state championships and became the best cross country team in America.

You'll be inspired by their young coach, who built a culture of greatness by teaching integrity, hard work, and commitment so their dreams could become reality.

And you'll learn how this coach prepared these young men for the challenges they would face later in life.

Coaching distance runners is something I have worked at and enjoyed for more than 50 years. I have been fortunate to coach more than 325 National Association of Intercollegiate Athletics (NAIA) All-Americans in cross country and track. I also served as the US men's distance coach for the 2005 IAAF World Championships in Helsinki, Finland, and the 2012 London Olympic Games, and as the US head coach for the men's cross country team at two World Championships: Boston in 1992 and Cape Town, South Africa, in 1996.

I met Coach Ron Martin when he brought his team from Caldwell, Ohio, to our running camp at Malone College, now Malone University, in the 1970s. That was the beginning of a lifelong association and friendship. He became one of my instructors at future camps because of his thirst for knowledge and his ability to motivate and to lead.

His career included working with me as an on-track marshal at the 1996 Atlanta Olympic trials, ushering all the winners around the track and on to the drug-testing facility. He accompanied me on multiple trips to Europe and Australia, leading and teaching young runners in international competition. Now, in semi-retirement, he has initiated and operates summer training camps for coaches to bring their teams at a nominal cost because he knows the value of such experiences. He told me this was his way of giving back to all the coaches who have mentored him and to all the athletes who have shared their knowledge with him. "I've preached giving back to every one of my athletes through the years," he said. "So starting the Team Camp of Champs may be the best thing I've ever done in this sport."

Ron is blessed with the amazing ability to empower people and teach them the right way to live. He instills positivity and has adopted the mantra of our friend, the legendary distance coach Dr. Joe Vigil: "When you believe in someone, you add value to their life." Ron is a model not only for coaches but also for anyone aspiring to be successful. I so appreciate his integrity, generosity, fairness, kindness, and true presence of humbleness, which championship coaches rarely have.

"Too small to win" was what many coaches thought as Caldwell moved themselves up to the largest school division races. Caldwell High School, with 340 total students, competed against teams that were often 5 to 8 times bigger. This story shows that regardless of what you pursue in life, size does not limit your potential for success. Get ready for a great read and a fascinating journey.

Jack Hazen

2012 US Olympic Distance Coach
Cross Country Coach Emeritus, Malone University

AUTHOR'S NOTE

You wouldn't think a tiny place like Caldwell, Ohio—a village with three traffic lights and a population under 2,000—would become a cross country hotbed. But in the 1980s, a group of young men from Caldwell banded together to become the best high school boys cross country team in the nation.

This book focuses on the Caldwell High School boys cross country team's rise from 1983 through 1986, the beginning of a dynasty. I am proud to have coached the program during those four magical years and the eight seasons leading up to them.

Throughout the book, you'll hear personal accounts from many of the remarkable runners who made it all happen, including members of the 1986 national championship team:

- Seniors: Tony Carna, P.J. Norris, Randy Lowe
- Juniors: Brian Norris, Stacy Huffman, Danny Lowe
- Freshman: Steve "Arnie" Ferguson

You'll also hear from Tom Ferguson (we know him as "Deuce"), Brent Marshall, and Brent Sells, who helped pave the way in the years leading up to that season. Quotes and insights from the runners, recounting some of their best memories and how this experience shaped them, are sprinkled throughout the book.

The purpose of this book is to show—to the greater community of cross country and track and field, and to sports fans at large—that there are many more facets to success than just athleticism. It takes commitment, not only to coach or teammates or program, but also to oneself, to be truly great.

While training and preparation were vital to our success, I believe our philosophy was just as important. Nothing was left to chance, and every practice had a purpose. We kept detailed notes of each practice session

Coach Ron Martin, Wife Bev, Son Christoper and Daughter
Heather before Easter Mass - March 1986

Coach Ron Martin

and posted the results of every workout so that each runner knew how he was doing; anyone who "loafed" a run or his training regimen heard about it. I wanted the boys to be confident but not cocky, and in the process, we built an extremely strong team culture.

You'll learn much more about how the boys and I battled through the growing pains of working together, building a team, upping the competition when it was necessary, and eventually accomplishing what we set out to do.

The book's chapters carry themes from some of the most meaningful sayings and bits of wisdom I've gathered during my cross country coaching career—themes that correlate with our rise to success. I've also included 10 "keys to success" throughout the chapters to highlight elements that were critical to our success.

However, this book is not at all about me, and I don't want it to be about me. Sure, you will learn many parts of my story, but this book is about those incredible young men who started a cross country dynasty.

You can have the very best training program in the world, but if you don't have the athletes to implement it, you're not going to be very successful. When I saw the boys buying in and putting in the work—not just showing up but quite literally going the extra mile—that's when I got excited.

While you'll hear from many different voices in the pages that follow, I want to give special recognition to Randy Lowe, a key team member from 1983 to 1986 who helped guide the book's development. Randy was really driven then, and still is. I am honored to coauthor this book with him.

My wife Bev has also been instrumental in her support. She not only raised our five children (Chris, Heather, Erica, Rachel, and Rebecca) but also served as a second mom to our runners at Caldwell. She had as much to do with the success of the Caldwell cross country program as anyone.

I have been blessed in my coaching career because of the relationships I've formed with my runners. These young men and women always made me proud, and they carried the habits they learned in cross country with them into their very successful personal and professional lives.

Together, they've embodied my mantra: "When excellence is in sight, good is not enough." I cannot thank them enough for allowing me to come along for the ride.

Ron Martin
Canal Winchester, Ohio, 2024

ABOUT CROSS COUNTRY

Cross country is about a lot more than running fast—it represents a true test of grit and determination.

Runners dash over hills, pass through woods, traverse creeks, cross beaches, and cover all manner of other types of landscape. Courses are marked off with things like flags and cones, tape or ribbon or chalk. Races—which are known as meets—typically start with open, level terrain before twisting and turning. Narrowed spots can cause runners to trip over each other's feet or elbow one another for position. Finishes involve a corral or chute.

Meets usually cover 5K, which is 3.1 miles, and participants run as individuals and teams. Results used to be tabulated by hand, but now they are all computerized, with runners wearing a computer chip on their shoe or within their bib. Using the right or wrong techniques can mark the difference between winning and losing. If you sprint out in front at the beginning of the race, you could burn too much energy and get gassed—and passed—in the final mile.

Team scoring requires the strategy and precision of an air traffic controller. Each team's first five runners count toward scoring, meaning the midrange or slower runners' results often dictate whether a team wins or loses a meet. As in golf, the lowest score wins. Races are scored by assigning a point value for the place a runner finishes, so, for example, the runner who finishes first scores 1 point, while finishing 55th would scores 55 points.

The best possible finish in a race is first through fifth, 1+2+3+4+5, which generates a "perfect score" of 15 points. The sixth and seventh runners on a team don't factor into the team total, but they are very important because they can displace scoring runners from other teams, making those teams' point totals higher. In the event of tying point totals, the sixth runner serves as the tie breaker.

Unlike other sports, where physical talent can create or diminish opportunities or where teams have limited roster sizes, everyone can participate in cross country, no matter their skill level. Undersized kids who may be deemed too small or too scrawny to play sports like basketball or football are welcome. That sense of belonging is one of the things that makes the sport so great.

Cross country requires athletes to ask more of themselves and their teammates, to motivate and support each other, to battle together against everything—foes, running surfaces, the weather, and any other limitations that could hold them back.

If each team member can stay aligned and buy into the greater goal, if they can follow the right training program and master proper running techniques, together they can accomplish the unimaginable.

XC

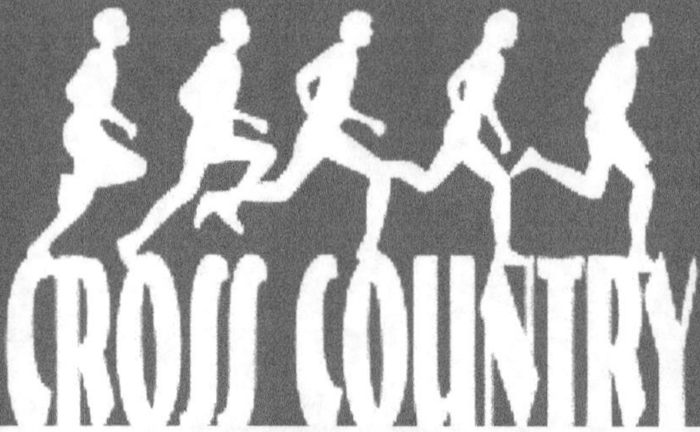

01.

SOMETHING HAD TO CHANGE: 1985

September 1985

As the yellow school bus creaked along the interstate, I kept wondering whether I'd made a huge mistake.

It was the start of the 1985 cross country season in Ohio, and our Caldwell High School boys cross country team, hailing from a tiny village in the Appalachian foothills, was attempting the unthinkable.

David vs. Goliath tales are one thing. But the underdog squad I coached was preparing to face off against 18 Goliaths at the same time.

Every mile on the three-hour bus ride—across the route's twists and turns, past the rolling hills and small towns—brought us closer to our moment of truth.

I had put my team in this impossible situation. In the previous two seasons, Caldwell fell just short—painfully, hauntingly short—of winning the state Class A cross country championship for small schools.

As the team's head coach, I hurt for the boys who had given their all. They devoted every ounce of their being to the team—the interval runs, the summer workouts, the hills, the sweat, the pain, the tears. They did everything I'd asked ... and they still lost.

It felt like we were cursed. And something had to change.

Instead of casually strolling through our schedule, I wanted our guys to get excited about *every mee*t and face more consistent challenges.

The way I saw it, to learn how to be the best, we had to face the best teams—and in the seasons prior, we had failed to reach our true potential because we hadn't been properly challenged during our regular season.

To remedy this, I decided to switch things up and face bigger schools. But my focus wasn't on the next level up, Class AA medium-sized schools. Instead, I was thinking about the big-school division, Class AAA—schools that were many times our size.

The best and most competitive teams ran at the Class AAA level. Some of these schools had 70–90 kids going out for cross country each year.

My team had 10 members.

Some of the runners, I'm sure, questioned my sanity—and I didn't blame them. I wondered about it myself as the bus made its way to Tiffin, my old stomping grounds, for our first meet against the massive schools. The meet was organized into two heats for the large Class AAA schools, and I had signed up Caldwell for the most competitive one, the "fast" heat, which featured 18 other entrants.

It was a lot to think about—but the bus ride didn't offer much chance for calm or clarity.

Since there was no AC on the bus, the windows were down, and the wind whipping through the windows made the ride about as loud as a jet engine. A boombox played music that you could almost make out.

Each person on the bus had a row of seats to himself—one benefit of having a small team—but given the noise and anticipation, it was tough to concentrate.

Our moment of truth was drawing near—the chance for the tiny school to prove itself against the big schools.

David dropped Goliath with a stone and sling, and Caldwell would battle Ohio's cross country Goliaths in hand-me-down racing spikes and shabby uniforms.

Still, I liked our chances. What this team lacked in swanky running gear and a fancy bus we made up for with something that no one could ever take away from us, something that would help us face any challenge: heart.

PART I
HOW IT ALL BEGAN:
1952-1982

02.

THE RACE WAS ON

Go! Go! Go! Faster!

It was a race against the clock, a sprint to the finish.

Breathe ...

Breathe ...

On June 17, 1952, in Lincoln Park, Michigan, a downriver suburb of Detroit, I was born in a car that was pulled over on the side of the road.

My parents had a plan for my delivery—but when my mother couldn't reach my father by phone after her water broke (he was at work managing a local grocery store), she wound up having her friend drive her to the hospital.

The friend sped to the hospital, darting in and out of traffic.

The race was on, and I was in a hurry—so much of a hurry, in fact, that they didn't reach the hospital before I was born. My entrance into the world was fitting, given that I would spend much of my life running along roads for cross country training.

I spent my early years in Michigan with my parents, my older sister, and my younger brother. We lived there until I was in third grade.

I remember riding a train to Tiffin, Ohio, my mother's hometown, to visit her relatives and disembarking at the train station at Fort Ball. Over time, my mother grew tired of traveling such a long distance, especially with three young children, to see her family. She wanted to live closer to home, and eventually she and my father decided to move there.

We lived in a two-story white house on Market Street across from San Mar, a small local pharmacy. Times were tough and money was tight, especially after my younger sister was born. I wore lots of hand-me-downs, including my older sister's blue jeans.

My parents divorced several years later, at which point my mother took us to live at our grandparents' house. They worked hard but didn't have much. And yet they would gladly give you the shirt off their backs, even if it was tattered and torn.

It was a full house. In addition to the five of us and my grandparents, four of my grandparents' other children also lived in the house. The eleven of us shared one bathroom, and four children crowded into one bed together to sleep.

I found an escape and an outlet in sports. My siblings and I played neighborhood games outside from dawn until dusk, when we had to come inside for meals and bedtime. Neighborhood games were loose and unstructured—no adult-organized activities, just free play. We played everything we could—football, basketball, baseball, hide-and-seek, and capture the flag.

In the summer, we fished, built rafts, and sailed along the Sandusky River. In the winter, we had epic snowball fights, went sledding, and made snow forts.

When the streetlights came on, my mother would stand out on the front porch, hands cupped around her mouth, calling our names. Even then, as we heard that familiar voice echo through the streets and alleyways, we didn't want to stop playing and go inside. We wanted to stay outside a little while longer. We didn't want to go to bed. Not yet.

When I was in sixth grade, my mom remarried. My stepfather took on the responsibility of taking care of our already-made family as if it were no big deal at all. He soon became my biggest cheerleader at sporting events. My eyes found him in every crowd during my games and meets. I remember him standing along the curve at track meets, yelling, "Feels good! Feels good!" as I passed by. He always tried to be positive and encouraged me to push myself and to do my best. And when my sporting events were finished, I would go find him and he would greet me with a smile and congratulate me on a job well done.

While I played many sports as a boy, I didn't discover the sport that would change my life until my sophomore year in high school, when my friend Dave asked me a life-changing question.

"Hey, why don't you run cross country?" he asked.

"Cross country?" I asked. "Is that running all over the country, or what?" I had no idea what the sport was all about.

"Not exactly," Dave said. "Come on, just come to one practice. Then you'll see."

I remember my first practice vividly. Summer hadn't fallen away quite yet, and it was still balmy. The runners were dressed in shorts and mismatched T-shirts. Some of the guys I knew, some I didn't.

In the other sports I had played, everyone had the same look, more or less – football guys were burly, and basketball players were tall. I was always told that part of having success in sports is based on chance, on the body you were born with.

But cross country wasn't like that. Different runners had different body types.

I happened to be tall and skinny.

I might have a chance at being good at this sport, I thought.

Coach Norm Grimes—a soft-spoken and devout man who became a missionary after his teaching career was complete—gathered up the runners and instructed the newcomers to run 3 miles while he and the rest of the team ran 10 miles.

We all started together. The plan was to have the newcomers run with the rest of the team until the 1½ mile mark, at which point we would turn around and head back to the school. Coach Grimes wanted us to start off easy.

"We have a long season ahead of us," he said.

We took off together, and I slipped right in with the seasoned runners. My new teammates watched me go and shook their heads in amazement. At the turnaround point, they encouraged me.

"Keep going! Keep going!" they said.

So I kept going.

I ran 10 miles that day. By the end of the run, I was dripping in sweat and shaking from exhaustion. My muscles buzzed ... but I couldn't help but feel proud.

I never realized how far I could run before.

I finished those 10 miles with our team's number one runner, Milt. My teammates grabbed me by the shoulders, cheered for me, and told me that I could make a huge difference on the team.

And I fell for it hook, line, and sinker.

I didn't *like* running at first, but I was good at it. As I continued practicing and got into better running shape, I started enjoying it more and more. We won our conference championship every year that I ran cross country, and by the time I graduated from Tiffin Columbian High School, I was a standout cross country runner.

With my affinity for the sport, I knew I wanted to run at the collegiate level. At first, I ran cross country for the Ohio State University, where, as a freshman, I was the third man on the team. In the fall of 1971, I worked with my teammates as a volunteer at the Ohio high school state cross country meet. That year, the state meet was held at OSU's Scarlet and Gray Golf Course. We worked in the finish line chute, keeping the finishers in the correct order.

One of the teams in the small school division race that day was Caldwell High School. Who would've thought that four years later, I'd be coaching at Caldwell?

I didn't stay long at Ohio State. The program I had been sold on during recruitment was not what I experienced. It simply wasn't the right school for me, and I didn't feel a connection to the coach or the school community. I needed somewhere smaller, with a more intimate, personalized feel.

Additionally, I couldn't afford to pay room and board anymore, which left me tethered to home.

I chose to continue my schooling and running at Heidelberg College (now Heidelberg University) in Tiffin, mostly because it was close to my parents' home. By living at home and not paying for campus food and housing, college became a lot more affordable.

And I could walk to classes and practice. I studied education and ran cross country and track.

But transferring schools—despite saving me money—came at a high cost. Per NCAA rules, I lost my athletic eligibility and had to sit out a full year.

While I could practice with the Heidelberg team, I couldn't compete in a cross country meet until fall of my junior year. That was hard. But overall, I was much happier at Heidelberg and graduated on time with a degree in K–12 Health and Physical Education.

I got my first taste of teaching and mentoring at a summer camp called Camp Pittenger near Tiffin. I started as a dishwasher and quickly became an archery and riflery instructor. That first summer was a blast! That camp helped me discover how much I enjoyed working with children and helped me realize that I wanted to teach and mentor kids for the rest of my life.

I worked at Camp Pittenger as my go-to summer job for eight consecutive years. That's also where I met my wife, Bev. We both worked at an Easter Seal camp for children and adults with special needs. We were responsible for leading activities, participating in the entertainment, and helping the campers any way we could—including bathing them, feeding them, and pushing their wheelchairs. When you do that kind of work for five weeks, you really get to know the true nature of people and what is in their heart.

Bev and I saw each other at our best and worst, and our passion for helping others drew us together. We got married in 1979 and are still married to this day.

My experiences at Camp Pittenger solidified my passion for teaching and coaching—but as I graduated from Heidelberg, I still wasn't quite sure what to do next.

I checked for job openings on the board outside the placement office at Heidelberg. As I scanned down the list, I noted a few schools that were local to the area. For some reason, my eyes stuck onto one name that I didn't recognize.

Caldwell?

I checked a map of Ohio. Caldwell was more than three hours away by car, in the southeast corner of the state, almost to the West Virginia border. How would I get there for an interview? I didn't even have a driver's license. I couldn't afford the insurance, let alone a car. There was no reason for me to ever take my driver's test if I wasn't sure when I would be able to buy my first car. Besides, walking and running was good enough for me. I was relieved when my friend Milt volunteered to drive me there.

As we drove through hills and increasingly winding roads on the way to Caldwell, I couldn't help but notice how different this part of Ohio looked compared to the northwest part of the state where I grew up. The scenery was beautiful, with the hills—mountains to me—surrounding the town.

Lowell Anderson, superintendent of Caldwell Exempted Village Schools, greeted us when we finally arrived at the aging red-brick high school. Having driven so far as my chauffeur, my friend was invited to join us in the interview. After some light questioning, the super-intendent drove us around town and gave us the history of the cross country program at Caldwell, whose team I had seen at the state meet just a few years prior. We then ventured out onto the country roads surrounding Caldwell, where he showed us the running routes that were used for cross country practice. I was struck by the challenging terrain and tried to imagine what it might be like to run those routes with my teams one day.

"Caldwell is a dry town," Anderson explained. "Alcohol isn't served anywhere in town. It's against the law."

From the look on my friend's face, he didn't seem to like that idea one bit. As a young man fresh out of college, maybe that should have bothered me, too. But I liked the fact that Caldwell was dry. It added to its appeal. I wasn't interested in drinking alcohol, especially if I was going to be coaching and mentoring young people.

"Your college loans will be forgiven, of course," Anderson explained, "since you'll be teaching in a low-income school district."

My friend and I exchanged a glance. Living in a small town like Caldwell, helping kids from backgrounds like mine, *and* getting my student loans forgiven?

It was all very enticing. I liked the small-town feel of the place, and it was far enough away from home to allow me to "break ties" and chart my own course.

I'd spent almost my entire college career living with my family because I didn't have the money to live in a dorm. It was time for me to be out on my own—to find my pace and run my best race. And the more I heard and saw about Caldwell, the more I fell in love with the village in this scrappy, working-class Ohio town.

After receiving three job offers, I decided to take the job at Caldwell, where I would be the freshman health teacher and elementary physical education teacher as well as the high school cross country coach. My starting salary, coaching included, was $7,200 a year before taxes. As Bev and I came from impoverished homes, having a stable paycheck was like hitting the lottery. It also helped us financially to have our college loans forgiven for teaching in a low-income school district.

Most of all, I was just happy to be coaching and teaching. But I had my work cut out for me as I took over Caldwell's cross country program.

03.

THE PAST PAVES THE WAY FOR THE FUTURE

Caldwell is about as big as a postage stamp. The village, located along the West Fork of Duck Creek in Ohio's Appalachian foothills, covers 0.90 square miles and has a population of less than 2,000 people. The county seat of Noble County, it was founded in 1857, and the population grew, little by little, after the railroad came through.

Caldwell built up around its courthouse. Factories and schools sprung up. Residents worked and went to church and raised their families in Caldwell, and their children did the same, and their children's children, too.

Downtown Caldwell features common small-town necessities with not much else: a post office, an optometrist, a hardware store, a few churches, a few schools, the courthouse, a grocery store, a bank, and three stoplights.

When I moved to Caldwell in 1975, there wasn't even a fast-food chain in town—you had to go to Marietta, about 25 miles south, or Cambridge, 20 miles north, for fast food. The movie theater downtown kept going in and out of business.

It used to be that you finished school and started work at a factory or coal mine. But over time the factories and mines started closing, and opportunities became harder to come by. Financial hardship was common—the poverty rate outpaced the state and national averages. Most residents had not graduated from college.

Forget thriving—in Caldwell, the focus was survival: making it through another day, one step at a time. It was the quintessential small town, long on tradition and values, a place full of hardworking, well-meaning people.

Given my own hardscrabble beginnings and humble means, I knew I was home when I moved to Caldwell to teach physical education and coach cross country.

But I faced a tall order. The cross country team I inherited was in disarray. I was the third coach to lead the program in three short years, meaning the team had endured a roller coaster of changes in coaching styles and approaches. Coming in, I knew we had work to do and issues to correct. Some of the runners had a poor work ethic and lacked discipline—and it was obvious from every angle.

After a meet in the middle of that first year, one of my runners came up to me, red-faced and grinning.

"I tackled him!" he bragged.

"I know! I saw you tackle him! What was that all about?" I responded.

"There was a guy that kept cutting the course right in front of me ... so I tackled him."

I couldn't believe what I was hearing and shook my head in disgust.

"Don't you realize that all you did was slow yourself down?! Why didn't you just focus on the race?" I asked.

The runner gave me a surprised look. His teammates seemed puzzled, too. "But coach, he was cheating!" he said.

"You can't control what other people do on the course," I told him. "The only thing you can control is how hard you run and how fast you get to that finish line."

"I taught my runners the right way to do things, both in competition and in training—and the rugged terrain in and around Caldwell helped me to start getting through to them. As I came to realize, Caldwell's landscape was perfect for a training run. The word "hilly" gets thrown around a lot, but those hills were more like mountains jutting from the landscape. We had access, in close proximity, to about 15 different trails and courses ranging from three to 10 miles long.

Some of the courses—like the Noble County Fairgrounds—were used for home cross country meets. Others made the runners climb and roller coaster up and down hills, running over gravel and paying close attention for oncoming cars.

The back way to Belle Valley, northwest of Caldwell's outskirts, was among the most brutal of our practice courses. The boys ran over unpaved stone and dirt roads with lots of twists and turns, leading to the potential for tripping. Every turn in the road presented a new hill and a new challenge.

The course took the runners up an elevation gain higher than the Empire State Building's 1,454 feet before a nice steady decline put the guys back out onto the highway and on the way back to the school.

The terrain in Caldwell was so much different than the conditions in Tiffin, where I was raised. There were some small hills on Tiffin's course, but Caldwell's courses had *mountains*. You couldn't go a mile in any direction in Caldwell without going *up*.

KEY TO SUCCESS
TEST THE TERRAIN
We didn't train on hills—we trained on mountains!
We were lucky to be in Appalachia, with some
treacherous terrain. We had numerous challenging
training courses. My runners loved that because
it made them better distance runners.

It helped to have some talented runners, too—which in turn motivated me. I didn't want to come in and mess up their chances for success. I didn't want to be the coach who took an elite competitor and rendered them average.

The talented runners on my early teams forced me to be the coach I am today because they motivated me to continue my cross country education. There's always new information out there, and fortunately for me, most distance coaches and runners are willing to share their ideas. I took the time to go to camps and lectures, spoke to top athletes and coaches, and tweaked the training program.

One year, the Ohio High School Track and Cross Country Coaches Clinic featured world-class runner Sebastian Coe of England and Peter Coe, his coach and father. They stood in front of a room full of coaches and spoke to us about running as we all listened intently. Afterward, I sat with Seb and his dad and grilled them for another hour. With my notebook pages full of notes, I found a nearby napkin to scribble on and filled that, too.

I asked Peter what specific training strategies he used with his son. What was his go-to workout? They had not covered the topic in their presentation.

"The 'secret sauce' for this one is *surging*," Peter said, patting his son on the back. "Athletes run the first half of a workout at mile race pace, then the second half at a faster-than-mile race pace." I furiously jotted down every word. If *surging* was good enough for these legends, then it was good enough for me and for my team.

I was like a sponge in those days. I soaked up as much information as I could from whomever I could and continued learning every year—then implemented the new strategies and put them to the test on Caldwell's hills. As a teacher, it was important to me that my runners learn along with me. I wanted them to understand the training strategies we were using and why.

I also wanted to keep the parents informed so they understood that they were an important part of our program. So every Monday, I passed out a handwritten newsletter that reviewed each runner's performance the previous meet. The newsletter also included information about the upcoming meet, such as the teams we would face, individual and team goals, bus times, and more details for overnight trips.

You would have thought there was prize money in those newsletters the way the parents and runners looked forward to them! I didn't realize how important the newsletter was to the runners until the occasional times when I didn't have it ready to distribute on Monday. They didn't let me off the hook, and I had to promise to bring it to practice the next day.

Coaching, in my opinion, is an extension of teaching. I love helping kids develop their skills and giving them the opportunity to put those talents on display. And being an elementary physical education teacher helped me as a cross country coach because it allowed me to scout out talented runners at an early age.

I tried to instill a love of running in my elementary students. As soon as they came through the gym door, they started running warm-up laps, and then they did some stretching and prepared for the activity of the day. If they did well in class, sometimes I allowed them to stay after class and run around the gym rather than go back to their classrooms. Kids would do anything to stay in the gym!

Most importantly, I never assigned running as a punishment. Instead, I used it as an incentive. For example, I allowed the winners of a game or activity to celebrate by running laps. That was really genius, if I do say so myself.

I taught the students the fundamentals of sports like football, basketball, bowling, wrestling, cross country, track, and gymnastics. I also gave them the opportunity to compete and demonstrate their skills through tournaments where the whole school came out and watched. I think that program stimulated their interest not only in cross country but also in other sports because they were able to put the skills they developed in physical education class to good use.

I also tried to hold special events throughout the school year where parents were invited to come and watch. We held a cross country championship each fall. In the winter, we did what I called a "superstars' competition." The superstars' competition was patterned after television shows like *Battle of the Network Stars*. The event was a fundraiser for the high school cross country program and featured 10 physical fitness or track contests, each with its own score that was added up in the end to determine the winning individual. It helped each child feel like they were a part of something special and important, which is exactly how I wanted all my students and athletes to feel.

In the spring, we did track and field. We always ended the year with a mini-Olympics at the local fairgrounds. We had events like the "math half-mile," in which students stopped midway through a race to do some math problems before sprinting to the finish. I added seconds to their times for any incorrect answers to the math questions. This really leveled the playing field and allowed some nonathletes to outshine the faster runners.

After watching satisfied parents, excited kids, and passionate future athletes leave the venue, I realized my talent for planning, analyzing, and strategizing to get the best out of my students. It dawned on me that I was already doing this in my coaching.

But building a successful program like the one I experienced at Tiffin Columbian High School took time. Success rarely happens as quickly as one might hope.

As I learned more about coaching, I came to realize how much we'd overtrained during my high school days. We ran about 13 to 15 miles a day—5 miles in the morning and then 8 to 10 miles at night—all for a two-mile race. As a result, we were leg tired by the end of the season.

With that in mind, I implemented a strategy for Caldwell's runners centered around peaking, which meant runners tapered off their workload during the end of the season, so their legs were less tired as they headed into district, regional, and state competitions.

Smart training and proper communication are essential to a team's success. I relied on my athletes to give me input on how they felt the day after a hard workout. It helped being in my 20s and early 30s at the time—I ran with the team for every distance run during the season and in the offseason mileage clubs, giving me the distinct advantage of also knowing how my own legs felt, too. If the boys were too proud to tell me that they were hurting, I could trust my own legs to tell me the truth.

My being able to run with the team helped me challenge the runners and build rapport with them. I wasn't just some coach barking orders and blowing a whistle. I could stick with our top runners, and on interval runs I was relentless, pushing the guys to dig deep when every instinct told them to slow down and coast.

My being out there, running alongside them, made it a lot harder for the runners to slack off and complain.

Through trial and error, research and results, I began to establish a system. As I incorporated new ideas and training methods each year, I gained more and more confidence in my own coaching abilities.

Perhaps the most impactful concept I introduced early in my coaching career was the mileage club: Over the summer, team members would try to run 500 miles or more in 60 days. Each runner had to run an average of 8.33 miles per day and no less than 5 miles at a time—which isn't much in the grand scheme of cross country. The purpose was to get the runners in great shape before the season even started so they'd be ready to jump right into the finer points of training, instead of trying to get into shape once the season had started.

Why 500 miles in 60 days? I had read an article on periodization and building endurance. According to the article, if you want to be a good cross country runner, you should train 2.5 times the distance you race. I did the math. Since we were racing 3.1 miles at every meet, I decided that our goal for 60 days would be 500 miles.

As an incentive, anyone who made the 500 Mile Club received a T-shirt and a mileage club trophy. Not everyone was able to successfully complete the mileage club, but those who did showed vast improvement. Even those who didn't make it improved from the many miles they had run.

Some might wonder if offseason training is worth all the effort. In my experience, it was absolutely critical to our success. If runners entered the season already in great shape, it was easier to build on their existing fitness and develop their energy systems, both anaerobic and aerobic.

The 500 Mile Club became a key feature that helped us reach the next level. We even added a winter mileage club to prepare for track season. I much prefer cross country to track, but track is important for all-year conditioning to create the best possible outcomes in cross country. The kids who ran track always came into cross country season with an advantage.

At some point, we changed our in-season training program to a three-week cycle because it's scientifically proven that after 21 days, your body adapts to the stress you put on it. Therefore, it is counterproductive to continue to stress the body in the same manner beyond three weeks. It's smarter to adjust the amount of stress—to change the interval workout or the amount of rest between intervals. So that's what we did.

By the time I had coached at Caldwell for almost a decade, I had learned so much about coaching strategies and even more about working with kids. My tool kit was full: the 500 Mile Club, peaking, three-week training cycles, and advice from lectures and clinics, such as the surging strategy from Seb and Peter Coe. I was energized by what I was learning and excited for the future.

All these things could have really helped my early Caldwell teams. It's a shame that I didn't know then what I know now. That's just how it is with new coaches. In all my years of coaching, I strived to build a team culture that would get the job done—one that would inspire the runners to do what it takes to be good every year.

Now I had the knowledge needed to tweak the training program for each group of athletes. In doing that, we were able to build consistency from year to year. We started to reload each year instead of rebuilding from scratch. That helped pave the way for the future and set the stage for what was to come.

KEY TO SUCCESS
TEST AND REFINE YOUR TRAINING PROGRAM

Past teams paved the way for the future.
If it weren't for the kids who ran for us from 1975
to 1982, the story of the 1983–1986 teams wouldn't
be worth telling. The earlier runners were
our guinea pigs and gave us the chance
to perfect our training program.

PART II
THE START: 1983

04.

SOMETHING SPECIAL BREWING

Six runners stood before me.

It was Caldwell's first official practice of the 1983 season, and we had only six runners. Six is a dangerously low number for a cross country team. There's strength in numbers. Seven runners typically make up a varsity squad. Your top five runners factor into scoring, and the sixth and seventh runners can help knock other teams' runners out of position. It's good to have backup just in case one of your runners is unavailable, gets injured, or can't finish the race.

To put it into perspective, large schools sometimes have 70–90 runners go out for cross country, and from there they can pick and choose the very best runners of the group. Our team's size represented less than 10 percent of some of the larger schools.

We searched high and low across Caldwell, trying to find anyone who might want to join our cross country team ahead of the 1983 season. We knew the turnout wasn't going to be great.

But six?

Not only would we have no safety net, but with only six runners, we would be required to run everyone at every race. There was no junior varsity, no B-team, no alternates, no resting, and absolutely no margin for error.

I'd previously had success with a small team like this one. But if you saw that ragtag bunch in the fall of 1983, you wouldn't have expected much. And you definitely wouldn't anticipate the makings of a dynasty.

That first practice was the moment when Caldwell's fortunes started to change, all because of two pint-sized freshmen who were in attendance that day: Tony Carna and P.J. Norris.

To be fair, Tony really wasn't a "new" runner. He started running at an early age—not for sport, but for the love of it. Before his family moved to Caldwell, Tony lived on a farm, and while his dad mowed the grass with one of those big riding lawn mowers that looked like a moon buggy, little Tony would run laps in the grass with his dog, Peanuts.

IN TONY'S OWN WORDS As a kid I ran everywhere. Walking was boring. Running came easy to me, and it was just a cool, fun thing to do.

When we moved to Caldwell I was in second grade, my dad took me out for a run. We ran to the fairgrounds, which was less than a mile away. My dad struggled on that hill, and he trained for two or three weeks before he took me back out for a run.

By fourth grade, Tony ran road races. By fifth or sixth grade, he traveled with the high school cross country team, riding the bus and hanging out with the older guys. At the time, there were no open races for the younger kids, so Tony made his own, trying to keep up with the high school guys. He was *hooked*. He was all in. Running was his life.

IN TONY'S OWN WORDS I already loved running, but when my dad took me to a home cross country meet in the late 1970s, I was amazed just watching the spectacle of it all. The coaches and families were cheering the runners on as they navigated their way through the hilly course. I couldn't believe it. It was perfect for me! I asked my dad how old you had to be to join. I had found my sport. When I started seventh grade, I weighed only 52 pounds, but unlike other sports, in distance running it wasn't a disadvantage.

When Tony came out for track in seventh grade, he ran the mile in 5:03—which tipped me off that he was shaping up to be a special runner. He cut his mile time further as an eighth grader. We considered having him run for Caldwell's high school team a year early because he would help the team immensely, but it would have cost him a year of eligibility. We ended up quickly scrapping that idea.

Tony was a special runner. He had talent, and people followed him. He was someone to build the team around. And his arrival for the 1983 cross country season marked the moment when everything started to change for Caldwell.

Tony set a different tone with his work ethic. If he was supposed to run five miles, he was running five miles—not four miles, not four and a half. He wanted to get better and push himself. As a quiet leader, he had a knack for making everyone around him better and drawing people in.

That was the case with a middle school acquaintance of his, P.J. Norris. P.J. and his younger brother Brian bounced around a lot during their childhood, living in Michigan and Florida before their family moved to Caldwell when P.J. was in seventh grade.

P.J. loved sports and was an all-around athlete—baseball, football, soccer, basketball, tennis, golf. You name it, he played it. After all the bouncing around, sports represented a way for P.J. to fit in and belong.

Tony and P.J. were in the same eighth grade science class taught by my assistant coach, and along the way, they became friends.

One day, Tony approached P.J. and asked him to come out for track. *Why not?* P.J. thought. He enjoyed all the sports he played, especially football. But he wasn't a big kid—he was probably 5-foot-7 and 120 pounds. He didn't think he was big enough to play football in high school, and he found himself at a crossroads, without a sport for his freshman fall sports season.

A week or two after the eighth grade football season ended, Tony approached P.J. again and asked him to run in the open race at the high school cross country league meet. The open race was mostly for kids who didn't make the varsity team or underclassmen still being developed.

Once again, P.J. thought, *Why not?*

IN P.J.'S OWN WORDS I agreed to do it without even knowing what cross country was! I had run track, so I figured it was something like that. In my mind, I'm thinking it was going to be like a steeplechase with kids running and jumping over hurdles and water hazards.

Tony goes out there that day and won the race by what I thought was a million yards. I finished second in the race, beating all of the junior varsity kids, despite not having really been running distance at all that fall. Having beat high school runners and understanding the sport a lot more by the end of the day, I decided I was done with football and I would go out for cross country. If Tony was going to be on that team, I would be on it, too.

Tony and P.J. matched up well with the three returning runners from the previous year's team—seniors Brent Marshall and Mike White and junior Tom "Deuce" Ferguson.

Brent was our top returning runner—he finished in sixth place at the 1982 state cross country meet and earned All-Ohio status. Heading into the 1983 season, Brent had the potential to be one of the top runners in the state. He was a pure, effortless athlete—he also played basketball—and he set a fast pace for the team.

Mike, our number two runner in 1982, left a deep impression on his teammates. He came to his first practice in jeans, since he didn't have running gear, and removed the insoles from his shoes because they made his feet hurt. He also used Cramergesic ointment, which is similar to Ben-Gay but much more powerful, to warm up the muscles. It is *very* warm—and it smells like liquid fire. One time, after he used his ointment, he wiped his hands on the towel that I showered with, and I didn't know it. I wiped my face with the towel, and it burned—a lot! The team still likes bringing up that story all these years later.

Deuce, meanwhile, was a natural leader and part of a long line of Ferguson runners. He was named after his father, Tommy. However,

Senior Brent Marshall

the family didn't feel like junior or "second" fit, so they went with Deuce, and to this day, many of his friends and family know him by that name.

Deuce grew up around the team. His sister and two older brothers were runners. When he was in sixth and seventh grade, he was our team manager, doing whatever was asked of him, including having water available, carrying sweats to the finish line, and anything else the coaches needed. Over the years, the little brother came into his own as a standout runner.

IN DEUCE'S OWN WORDS My family had to move because my father had lost his family-owned business. It was a struggle at times, but what kept me going was the camaraderie that Ron and Bev had built with this team. I didn't feel as lonely. That's why I felt a loyalty to that group and also the loyalty to help others.

With money tight, Deuce and his siblings used their own money for items like jeans and shoes, and he wore his one pair of Brooks Varus Wedge running shoes everywhere. He'd wear them to school, change into his running clothes, and practice or race in the same pair of shoes.

That well-worn feel applied to our team uniforms, too—they were half a dozen years old at that point. Team members ran and sweat in them, year after year. Then the uniforms were washed, holes were sewn up, lengths were adjusted to fit the next person who needed them, and they were worn again the next year.

IN DEUCE'S OWN WORDS A combination of financial struggles and small-town insecurities created self-doubt and a feeling of being judged. This produced a drive and motivation to succeed in running and also life. Even though we had very limited resources, all five of us Ferguson children went to college.

Deuce found purpose—and a steady foundation—in cross country. Of the returning runners, he was the most committed to the program's success. He participated in the 500 Mile Club, our offseason training program, as an eighth grader. That's just how the Fergusons were. It didn't matter the time or year or the weather. It could be snowing and below zero or it could be scorching temperatures. Deuce was out there running every day.

Having Brent, Mike, and Deuce returning reassured me. Those three were experienced runners and a good group to build around.

In addition to the three returning runners, junior Brent Sells—whom Deuce had introduced to cross country—was in his first year. Brent had run track for a year but primarily looked at cross country as training for basketball. He was a talented player on the high school basketball team and wanted to improve his fitness levels to help his play.

Our summer workouts gave me optimism. Championships are made in the offseason, and we ran hard. We ran a lot. Four of the runners achieved the 500 Mile Club with me—Deuce led the way at 525, followed by Tony (512), Sells (505), and Mike (502).

Successful teams are made when no one's looking. The more you do something, the better you're going to be at it. If you want to be a better piano player, you practice playing the piano. And if you want to be a better runner, you practice running. This offseason training allowed our guys to build a base so we could start interval and speed workouts much earlier in the season.

KEY TO SUCCESS
SUCCESS STARTS IN THE OFFSEASON

It takes drive, determination, and dedication
to succeed, and that work starts in the offseason.
We had all three. The runners did the 500 Mile
Club twice a year, and most of them completed it.
Even those who didn't complete it benefited
from the miles they put in.

Our location definitely shaped our success. The runners turned hilly Caldwell into their own course. They'd run along the sidewalks and through neighborhoods, over bridges and across streets. When they ran on the roads, they tried to face traffic as much as possible to avoid getting hit by cars. We paid close attention to shift changes at the local plant, too, when traffic picked up as workers rushed to leave.

Nothing compared to the Caldwell Cemetery, which sits on a hill overlooking the town. The team used the cemetery for training and interval workouts. The quarter-mile loop was perfect for interval runs, and the last straightaway was slightly downhill and through the woods. It had a beautiful setting, hassle-free environment, and challenging terrain. I would stand on the ridge and monitor the runners' pacing.

The guys were always cognizant and respectful of the plots, taking care not to step on any graves. On those runs through the cemetery, surrounded by granite and ghosts, our team came alive.

That was also the year I started having team members run the entire course before a meet. It probably seems counterintuitive to run the course before the race, but I wanted the team to be prepared for every part of it: every twist, every turn. Not all courses were well marked, and I wanted us to avoid surprises like holes, hills, and turns. Running the course before a race also allowed us to get in additional mileage for the day.

The extra running would leave the team better conditioned, and things wouldn't feel so new, which was important for a young, unproven team. It could also be intimidating for other teams to see Caldwell's team running three miles before a race like a well-oiled machine.

We might not win, but no other team was better prepared. So I approached 1983 with a good feeling about our chances. Ahead of the season, even with only six runners, I had a lofty goal in mind: to win the Class A Ohio state cross country meet.

Maybe I was being foolish. Or maybe I could sense something special brewing.

05.

THE REAL DEAL

Runners crowded at the starting line in anticipation while their stomachs, full of butterflies and nervous energy, did somersaults.

BANG!

The gun sounded, and Caldwell's "Six Pack" was off, a flurry of legs and arms and hopes and dreams. It was the first meet of the 1983 season, the Newcomerstown Invitational, a firm and fast course we'd run several times in previous years. It was so fast, in fact, that we often joked that it might be a little short of the typical 3.1-mile race distance.

With only half a dozen runners on our team, we needed everyone to do their best. We were like a tightrope walker without a safety net. The margin of error was razor thin. One false step, one twisted ankle, one stumble, and that would be it.

With no depth to the team, an injury to even one boy—or heaven forbid, somebody quitting the team—would be disastrous. Our runners had quite a bit to learn. Tony was still a small, scrawny kid. He could keep pace with anyone, but he struggled to close—he was all lungs and no legs. He had to build up his strength. P.J., meanwhile, was completely new to the sport and was still learning the ins and outs of cross country.

As was typical for me, I was all over the course during the race, running from point to point, writing down split times and shouting encouragement to my runners. It helped that I had a deep, strong voice with a low tone—and from all of my feedback in practice, the runners could pretty easily pick up my bellow among all of the other coaches yelling for their runners.

Marshall led the Caldwell charge, setting a fast pace and challenging rival Tuscarawas Valley's top runner, John Sponaugle. Marshall kept with him for the first two miles before Sponaugle sped away. Second place was a strong showing for our top runner.

Tony—our freshman phenom—was running right behind him with a third-place finish, pushing Marshall to dig deeper and run harder. We had a powerful one-two punch with our established senior and our young gun. Tony had something to strive for while also working to bring out Marshall's best effort.

The fact that Marshall and Tony were matching each other stride-for-stride wasn't a surprise. What did surprise me was P.J. At one point during the race, I noticed he'd passed Deuce for our fourth spot; then he passed Mike for our third spot.

For someone still learning the ins and outs of cross country, he was giving me a lot of hope for the years ahead.

IN P.J.'S OWN WORDS When that gun went off, it was something else. I didn't really know where I was, but I just started picking people off—specifically, I found my teammates and started to pass them. I just kept going and going. By the end of the race, I passed everyone on the team except for Tony and Marshall. I was the third Caldwell runner across the finish line and finished seventh overall in my first-ever high school race.

That was the turning point for me. Coming into the season, I thought I was going to be the last guy on the team, and most races that year, I was our third runner. I went from sixth to third overnight. That taught me I could do it. Then in practices, I was running ahead of Mike White on a pretty regular basis. I realized I didn't have to go out as slow as I did. I knew I could race with or beat Mike. That changed my trajectory for the rest of that year and going forward.

Senior Mike White

Mike and Deuce rounded out our top five, finishing 14th and 17th, respectively. Our sixth and final runner, Sells, had the race of the day. He finished three seconds behind Deuce, yet his time was better than every other team's third-place finisher!

What we lacked in number of runners we were making up in quality.

IN SELLS'S OWN WORDS I'd never run a meet, so I just tried to stay close to Deuce. The first couple hundred yards, I was like, *Man, this is too fast, I'm not gonna survive*. But I finished right behind him.

Caldwell finished with a score of 43 points, well ahead of the second-place team, which scored 80 points. In its first race of the season, the Six Pack showed that it was quality and not quantity that would win the day, and we were coming for all of our competitors.

We'd passed our first test. And even with only six runners on the team, I felt oddly good about our depth. The team was committed to the program and their improvement and to their teammates.

That commitment carried through to the biggest early test on our schedule, the Tiffin Columbian Invitational in northwest Ohio, my old stomping grounds. The event, also known as the Tiffin Cross Country Carnival, was the 2nd largest high school invitational in the nation, attracting top runners from every corner of Ohio.

The Class A division had 20 teams, and the competition was among the best we'd face all year.

It was a lot for the team to take in, and I could sense their stress building. They were pressing. They were nervous. Ahead of the race, I wanted to keep things light and help them loosen up, which is why I stocked up the bus with roll after roll of toilet paper. Sheriff Carl Runion, who lived near the race site, was a family friend and all-around great guy—the Andy Griffith of Tiffin—and I thought he would get a laugh out of the team "decorating" his yard. We didn't want him to see us, so I made sure we parked the Caldwell High School bus out of sight the night we arrived.

He had vowed that he would catch us. He even bought a dog, Rambo, and put it in the backyard. But we knew Rambo wouldn't hurt a fly.

I don't know how many rolls were used, but it was a ton of them, and he didn't catch us that night. Somebody even put a bicycle in the tree. Some of the runners thought I was crazy, saying, "We're gonna go to jail if this keeps up." But you've got to know Carl Runion to know what you can and cannot get away with, and toilet papering his house became a tradition every time we went to Tiffin. It also set the tone for the weekend—we couldn't be caught.

When we arrived at Hedges-Boyer Park on race day, the rows of school buses and colorful team tents made it seem like we really were entering a carnival!

I always wanted my runners to perform well at Tiffin because it was my hometown, and our family and friends (especially Bev's dad, my stepdad, and my sister, Bette Ann) always came out to watch us and cheer us on. Like the course at Newcomerstown, the Tiffin course was mostly flat, but it was a little more difficult because the runners had to cross a creek.

The Carnival was the measuring stick to see how teams stacked up at the beginning of the season.

While the overall time of the race was much slower than the previous week, this didn't seem to affect us as much as it did the other teams. Putting on an amazing demonstration of cross country running, we had five runners finish among the top 10, with our sixth runner coming in a very respectable 21st place out of 127 runners in the Class A race. Even more amazing, Tony and Marshall finished in a dead heat for first place. They hit the tape together, but the race officials gave Tony the win by a tenth of a second.

As far as team points, Caldwell's total of 26 easily defeated the rest of the field. The second-place team had 114 points. As *The Journal-Leader*, Noble County's weekly newspaper, noted, "For the Redskins to outscore their opponents by the margin they did shows them to be among the cream of the crop when it comes to high school squads in the state."[1]

Our small team of mostly newcomers was the real deal.

That same day, Caldwell grade schooler Steve "Arnie" Ferguson—Deuce's younger brother—won Tiffin's Elementary One Kilometer Race, outrunning the entire field. It was exciting to think ahead to the day when he would join our high school team and run beside Tony, who began establishing himself as a star and a team leader over the course of the 1983 season.

Tony had talent—that was obvious from a young age—but more than that, he didn't take it for granted. He easily could have rested on his laurels and followed the seniors, who were known to slack off in practice. No one would have blamed him if he did. He still would have been an elite high school runner.

---

1 "Caldwell Runners Capture Tiffin Invitational Crown," *The Journal-Leader* (Caldwell, OH), September 15, 1983. Caldwell's school team name during the 1980s was the Redskins, a term for Native Americans that is widely considered offensive today. In recent years, sports teams such as Washington NFL team (now the Commanders) and Cleveland's Major League Baseball team (now the Guardians) have stopped using Native American mascots and nicknames. We've kept the name in a handful of quotations throughout the book but have minimized references due to shifting sensitivities and cultural norms.

If anything, Tony's teammates slacking off made him dig in deeper. He was going to show the others what dedication looked like. His goal was to be the best. And P.J. followed Tony's lead, doing everything he could to keep pace and pushing Tony.

P.J. helped the team in another big way, too. Recognizing our need for a seventh runner, he took it upon himself to recruit classmate Randy Lowe, whom he knew from school and church.

IN P.J.'S OWN WORDS Six runners weren't enough, and the Six Pack would only get us so far. At a minimum, we needed a full team. I knew Randy Lowe from school, junior high track, and church. I thought he would be a good fit. He got good grades and wasn't involved in other sports, so I took it upon myself to ask him to join us. I had no idea what kind of runner he could be, but I knew he was our kind of person.

Randy was the oldest of seven children. The boys shared one room, and the girls shared another. His family moved to Caldwell in the summer of 1978, just before he entered the fourth grade. His father was a coal miner at American Electric Power's Central Ohio Coal, home of the Big Muskie, at one point the world's largest dragline excavator, at nearly 22 stories tall.

It seemed like Randy was always working. The older kids did the dishes, forming an assembly line of sorts, and they also changed a lot of diapers. He and his brother had a paper route and collected and cut firewood. Randy's dad was part owner of a restaurant with a mini-golf course, and Randy mopped floors and maintained the golf course. He also helped his dad install insulation and aluminum siding. At school, he sold Little Debbie snack cakes for some extra spending money.

Times were tough, especially when his father's union went on strike over fair wages and his family relied on food stamps to keep all of those mouths fed. The summer of the strike, food staples for Randy's family were government cheese, peanut butter, and rice, along with lots of chili.

A lot of families in Caldwell struggled and were a paycheck away from trouble. That's just how it was.

Randy, like a lot of the runners, was on the smaller side. He felt like a punching bag for the eighth graders on the football team and ended up quitting football. He also participated in junior high track.

Randy's work ethic and resilience were visible as soon as he joined the team. He wasn't one of the most talented runners on the team—and we didn't need him to be. We needed more heart, and he had lots of it.

Since Randy joined the team late and hadn't gone through summer conditioning, he was far behind the other runners at the start of his career. He also had to sit out the first few races, per state rules. But given his dedication and commitment, I knew he would catch up and contribute in due time.

IN RANDY'S OWN WORDS Things weren't always easy when I first joined cross country. The older guys weren't very kind to me because I broke up the Six Pack. The seniors on the team would take my hat during practices and throw it somewhere along the course so I would have to run farther to retrieve it. Things like that made me consider whether or not I wanted to be a part of the team.

However, Ron and some of the younger guys on the team were very inclusive, which kept me going in the early days.

I ran a tight ship, but I made sure to keep things loose, too. I'm a prankster, and I would find ways to poke good-natured fun at everyone on the team, myself included. At an awards ceremony, I bestowed P.J. with a "Forgetful Award" due to his habit of losing things.

I also made them laugh by using my large nose to make a point.

"The nose knows," I'd tell my runners.

On rainy-day runs, we'd often splash each other in puddles just for fun. And I would post workout results on the wall with funny comments and pictures next to runners' names.

Life was hard enough. I wanted the runners to love running the way I loved running. I wanted them to feel that coming to practice was the best part of their day, and I wanted to provide them with a warm and supportive environment.

KEY TO SUCCESS
HUMOR
Setting the right tone and finding ways
to joke around with the runners helped to
build rapport and keep things light.

I wanted them to bring out the best in themselves and each other—and over the course of the 1983 season, Caldwell's talent and cohesiveness started to emerge. At one home dual meet against Fort Frye High School at the Caldwell Fairgrounds, we were running only five boys—Marshall did not race—and we still made sure that nobody broke into our ranks at the finish. Reminiscent of the 1966 Le Mans auto race in which all three Fords crossed the finish line side by side at the front of the pack, all five Caldwell runners came across the finish line together but were given official finishing places of one through five, for a perfect score of 15.

Our home course had a big hill that runners went over twice during the race. While the team ran as a group, it took some of our guys going up the hill a second time to all catch up to each other.

When Caldwell's last runner passed Fort Frye's first runner, the other runner whimpered, "Oh God," as he tried to catch his breath and muster up the energy to climb the hill. Ever since, we've called that hill "Oh God Hill."

As far as sheer numbers go, the biggest race of the season was the Malone College Invitational, held in Canton, over an hour north of Caldwell. Unlike Tiffin, it included a mix of high school and collegiate races. In the 1983 race, Caldwell competed against 25 other teams—and more than 170 other runners.

Among those other teams was McDonald High School, the reigning Class A Ohio state champions. McDonald was located in the northeastern part of the state, midway between Cleveland and Pittsburgh. Their team was led by Jim Stitt, who'd finished just ahead of Marshall in the state meet the prior season. I felt excited to see how our Six Pack stacked up against them.

Malone's course was a blend of both flat and hilly terrain. The first mile was pretty flat, but the next two were very hilly, making this one of the most challenging courses the boys ran on all year. The weather on race morning was fair, with a temperature in the mid-40s, somewhat ideal for a 5K race.

Putting "a firm grip on establishing themselves as the number one Class A squad in the state this year," as the *The Journal-Leader* reported[2], we captured the win relatively easily, with three runners among the first nine across the finish line. Marshall finished in second place, with the two freshmen, Tony and P.J., in fourth and ninth place, respectively. Mike came in 13th, and Deuce completed the rout as the fifth Caldwell runner across the finish line, in 24th place. The team's total of 52 points allowed us to easily defeat Perry, located near Lake Erie, which scored 147 points for second place.

Sells, running sixth, also had an excellent race, finishing ahead of Perry's last three runners (30, 32, 36) by crossing the finish line in 29th place. We advanced to a 63–0 record on the season.

> IN TONY'S OWN WORDS It wasn't until the Malone Invitational where we faced a lot of stiff competition, and we saw our guys responding to the challenge and continuing to improve, that I felt like we were capable of doing something really special.

Malone was also Randy Lowe's first race as a freshman, and it was a good one for a newcomer. He placed 146th out of more than 170 runners. He went on to run every race over the rest of the season, improving at every outing.

As we reached the halfway point in the season, the boys were getting comfortable running with and against each other, and their connection grew stronger and stronger as the year went on. Groups of red-uniformed Caldwell runners flew by, bunched together in synchronicity, and it was a beautiful thing—poetry in motion.

---

2 Ibid.

Team members like P.J. also learned more about the sport and how to optimize their performance. Initially, P.J. would just run as fast as he could, but that's an easy way to burn yourself out and fade in the final mile. Over the course of his freshman season, he became a stronger, more confident runner. Pacing himself off Tony took away some of the guesswork. If P.J. could keep Tony in his sights, he was going to have a good day.

It did my heart good to witness P.J. and the others buying into the program and becoming fully committed to improvement and to their teammates. It's easy for kids to lose their love of a sport, and so many factors can contribute to that, from coaches and teammates to playing time, parents, girlfriends, and grades. Seeing the team's dedication had me doing cartwheels inside. These kids were going to be a force. I could feel it.

IN P.J.'S OWN WORDS The beautiful thing about running and the thing that it taught us is that there's no referees, it's nobody else's fault. Either you produce or you don't. Period. It's the simplest thing in the world. There's no one to save you in running. It exposes all of your strengths and weaknesses. It teaches you that if you're willing to put in the work, it doesn't matter how tall you are, how slim you are, how nice your uniform is, or what kind of gear you have. None of that matters. If you put in the work consistently over time, you can win.

As the weather changed, cold and flu season kicked in, and the team continued to train outside, even in the rain and the cold. I frequently reminded runners to take their vitamin C and get some rest to help them avoid getting sick.

The Tipp City–Bethel Invitational was up next on the horizon. Sixteen teams entered the invitational, but it turned into a two-team race between Dayton Christian and Caldwell.

Dayton Christian was located clear across the state, not far from the Indiana border. Their team had the type of culture we were starting to build and a little bit more experience than our team. They were also led by senior Ken Petty, probably the best Class A runner in the state. The

1983 Team: Front L To R Deuce Ferguson, Mike White, Brent Marshall,
Brent Sells **Back L To R** Assistant Coach Dugan Hill,
Randy Lowe, Tony Carna, P.J. Norris, Head Coach Ron Martin

year before, we finished just ahead of them in the state meet. But while
we were building and growing, they reloaded behind Petty.

Heading into races, we didn't typically focus on other teams, but we
knew going into the race that Dayton Christian was tough. That was the
point of going to meets in every corner of the state—we wanted to see
our state competition first. It would have been easy to just stay in our
backyard and go undefeated heading into the state meet each year, but
that wouldn't have done us any good.

Petty was as good as advertised in the invitational, zipping past the rest
of the field to take medalist honors. Marshall placed second, 10 seconds
behind Petty; P.J. placed sixth; and Dayton Christian's David Rapp finished
seventh. With the first two runners from each team having crossed the
finish line, the score was deadlocked at 8–8.

IN RANDY'S OWN WORDS It was the closest invitational we had in '83. P.J. was second man and Tony was third man. As they came around the bend, and there was 600 meters to finish through a field, it just seemed like it was Caldwell–Dayton Christian, Caldwell–Dayton Christian. It just seemed like it was 1-2, 1-2.

The next four runners to finish were separated by a mere 20 seconds. Tony came in 10th place, 14 seconds ahead of Ben Johnson for the Warriors. Mike finished five seconds behind him, followed by Dayton Christian's Tim Wyatt just one second later. We held a two-point lead, 30–32. It all came down to one more runner.

Junior Deuce Ferguson accepting an award.
Coach Ron Martin standing in background

Senior Mike White accepting an award

With Dayton Christian on his tail, Deuce raced toward the finish line. He captured 14th place, three places and 11 seconds ahead of the competition.

Deuce's effort locked in the victory for us and kept our undefeated streak—103–0—alive by the narrowest of margins. Dayton Christian was a good team, and we beat them by 5 points even when some of our guys didn't run their best race.

We expected to face them again in the state meet. And if we could win now, with runners sick with colds, it made me hopeful about how we would race against them in November with the championship on the line.

Caldwell faced another unexpected test the following week at a quadrangular meet we hosted, the Caldwell Classic at Wolf Run State Park, that featured a tough Warren team. P.J., who'd developed into our regular third runner, sat this one out to visit his dad, who'd had heart bypass surgery at the Cleveland Clinic. This meant we needed strong finishes from everyone in order to remain undefeated.

The race was nip-and-tuck the whole way. Brent and Tony finished first and third, but Warren took second, fourth, and sixth to tighten things up. Mike placed eighth, tying the event at 12–12.

Warren took a one-point lead when its fourth runner placed ahead of Deuce. But Sells was there to save the day for us, finishing 11th—three paces ahead of Warren's fifth-place runner—to give us the win with 33 points to Warren's 35.

Our undefeated streak remained intact!

We wrapped up our regular season with a perfect 111–0 record. Everything had gone according to plan for the Caldwell boys. Now, our "second season"—the postseason—was here. And we just wanted to keep the momentum going.

06.

EVERY PLACE COUNTS

The postseason has a distinct feel, and not just because of the crisp fall air. The energy is different. The stakes are higher. More is demanded and required. Everyone is *tired* by this point—it's a long season, after all. The postseason is a time to push past the physical and mental challenges of a long season and ask a little bit more of yourself.

All of our training and preparation led to this moment.

After completing our regular season with an undefeated record, Caldwell was more than ready for the district meet held in late October in Cambridge, Ohio. The race involved 13 teams, all of whom we had defeated previously.

We didn't underestimate the race—we didn't underestimate *any* race—but as heavy favorites, we felt confident about the team outcome. The most heated aspect of the meet was the race for first place among the individual runners. Fighting it out for medalist honors were a couple of Marshalls, Matt from Bridgeport High School and Caldwell's Brent (who are not related despite having the same last name).

It was a photo finish, but when the final times were announced, Matt Marshall had crossed the finish line two-tenths of a second ahead of Brent Marshall. By the slimmest of margins, Brent Marshall missed winning his fourth consecutive race.

As far as the team competition went, it was another typical race, with our first five runners all bunched at the front of the pack. Tony came in fifth and P.J. finished ninth, while Mike and Deuce finished four seconds apart in 12th and 13th. That gave us a total of 40 points, which allowed us to easily defeat second-place Zanesville Rosecrans and its 71 points.

The following Saturday was the state meet, the day everyone had been waiting for. Ahead of the state meet, we began to strategically taper our workouts a bit, focusing more on speed work and less on miles. I wanted the team to be fresh and fast for the most important meets of the year. I felt we were looking good—strong and fast—headed to Columbus for the Ohio High School Athletic Association State Cross Country Meet.

As a coach, the lead-up to the state meet is a juggling act—a mix of strategizing about the course and understanding the strengths and weaknesses of competitors, figuring out the right race tactics to help the team succeed, motivating runners with well-timed comments and expectations for their results, and getting the runners ready but keeping them fresh.

You wonder if you've done everything you can, if you could have trained differently. You focus on the race itself while also recognizing that your team has been running this race for months already and that the offseason training and in-season adjustments will have already largely decided the outcome.

The team and I discussed some strategy before the race, and I gave each of them an idea of where I thought they might finish in the field.

The 12 best teams in Class A entered the race, but the favorites were the defending champions from McDonald, the always-strong team from Dayton Christian, and our undefeated squad. We felt good about our chances.

IN P.J.'S OWN WORDS I didn't really know much about how we stacked up against teams in the rest of the state. I knew we were good because we were winning races and I was coming home with trophies and medals. That was a bunch of fun! To some extent, it started to hit me around the district and state meets that year, because that's when we started to get some press and recognized in the rankings. The state meet was the first time I felt real pressure.

The weather on race day was not the best. It was cloudy with a temperature in the mid-20s, made just a bit chillier by 15 mph winds. The race took place on a 3.1-mile course at the Biggs Athletic Facility on the Ohio State University campus. Where many cross country courses are picturesque, incorporating hills and forests and passing near bodies of water, this course was basically just a big field that was dubbed "the cow pasture" because the runners and spectators had to avoid the cow dung patties scattered across it.

But even with the wind, the cold, and the cow patties, every team had to run in the same conditions, and I felt we were the best-conditioned team in the pack.

We arrived at the course early and went through our normal routine—jog the entire course, stretch well, warm up, and prepare to race. The state title was on the line. We were focused. We were ready to run.

The gun went off and the runners sped off the starting line. We didn't get off to a great start, yet I was confident the team would find their way and work toward the front of the pack. The race seemed to go by in a flash. It was difficult for me to navigate the course and the crowd while the race was going on. It wasn't a great spectator course. But I could see enough to know it was going to be close—really close.

As he had done all season, our senior star Brent Marshall led the way for us and finished in third place (Dayton Christian's Ken Petty finished first). Tony came in 13th, Mike in 21st, and P.J. in 27th. McDonald had four runners in the top 20. We had only two.

This race, however, really came down to how the fifth and final runner on each of the three leading teams finished. With the first four runners across the finish line, the scores stood at McDonald, 46; Caldwell, 64; Dayton Christian, 64. Then Deuce crossed the finish line in 32nd place without any McDonald runners in sight.

The Journal-Leader best described what happened next, after a last-minute burst from one of the McDonald runners: "Heading into the final mile, [McDonald's Tom] Kilborne was stationed in 57th place, and it appeared that Caldwell had a comfortable margin for victory. But the McDonald

Top Senior Brent Marshall Finishes 3rd Place at State Meet
Above Freshman Tony Carna Finishes 13th Place at State Meet

Deuce Ferguson finishing strong, Asst Coach Hill Timing

runner put together a stretch run that enabled him to move up nine places, including five in the last fifty yards."[3]

Deuce's strong finish brought our total to 96 points. But Kilborne's incredible sprint allowed him to cross the finish line in 48th place, giving McDonald a team total of 94 points. Dayton Christian's fifth runner came across the finish line in 34th place, for a team total of 98 points.

In the closest Ohio state cross country race in nearly half a century, the first three teams were separated by a mere four points. The Caldwell boys had run a great race against top competition, but came up short.

After such a close finish, I was wracked by the *what ifs*. What if Marshall had won the race? What if our freshman duo of P.J. and Tony had performed at their norm? What if we'd have practiced harder? What if I had coached them a little bit differently?

---

3 "McDonald Nips Redskins for Class A Title," *The Journal-Leader* (Caldwell, OH), November 14, 1983.

I'm sure the boys from Dayton Christian had their own *what ifs*. But sometimes you just have to tip your hat to an outstanding opponent. Tom Kilborne's race down the home stretch was one of those fantastic finishes that are talked about for years. All you can do is congratulate such a worthy opponent and use the *what ifs* as motivation for next time.

You can't control how other teams run, only your own destiny. I pride myself in knowing that our kids put their best on the line at the state meet. Looking back, it wasn't that we ran poorly. But losing by such a small margin really stung, and the tears and anger flowed.

With a record of 133–1, Caldwell had enjoyed our best season and best finish in the state meet since winning the state championship in 1973.

We had come so close with our ragtag group. But it wasn't enough. Even with the disappointing final outcome, the future was bright for Caldwell—and our success made people take notice.

People like Brian Norris (P.J.'s brother) and Danny Lowe (Randy's brother), both eighth graders who attended the state meet together, witnessed the guys coming down the chute and the pandemonium of a big race.

Front L to R Randy Lowe, Tony Carna, Deuce Ferguson, Brent Sells, Mike White
Back L to R Assistant Coach Dugan Hill, Head Coach Ron Martin

Banner Holders L to R Jill Devol, Amy Anderson **Front L to R** Randy Lowe, Deuce Ferguson, Mike White, Brent Sells, P.J. Norris **Back L to R** Assistant Coach Dugan Hill, Tony Carna, Brent Marshall, Head Coach Ron Martin

IN BRIAN'S OWN WORDS We were sitting on the bleachers. The race had just ended, and my adrenaline was running high after watching my first state meet. Danny turned to me and said, "Hey, I think I'm going to run next year." I said, "I am too. That was awesome." Before this day I had never given two thoughts about running in high school. In all honesty, it just hadn't entered my mind yet. But in that moment, after seeing the energy and excitement of a state meet finish and knowing P.J. and Tony were coming back, it was a no-brainer.

Danny and Brian vowed to come out for the team the following season. They wanted to be a part of what we were building. We had a returning team that was young, tough, and prepared to galvanize around Tony. We had a lot to look forward to.

PART III
THE BUILD: 1984

07.

BAND OF BROTHERS

Teams often think of themselves as a family. But Caldwell's 1984 team, with its older and younger brothers, strong bonds, selflessness, and parental support, really was one.

IN TONY'S OWN WORDS To understand this team, you have to think of us not as kids from the same town but as brothers. We would compete against each other and then defend each other furiously. Every single interval, we competed. If someone caught you, you wanted to get them the next time.

Having that brotherly relationship, we could be brutal and brutally funny at the same time, and still get away with it. There was a line, and everyone knew where it was. We'd kid each other about girls or getting outkicked by some guy with terrible form. It was brutal, but we were laughing together.

Their backgrounds played a role. Times were tough, and money was hard to come by. Their home lives were complex; some were abusive. Some of their parents had a hard time putting a meal on the table every night.

Unfortunately, I didn't realize how bad some of them had it until much later, when they opened up a little more.

They weren't running just to run, and it wasn't some chore or obligation, either. Running represented opportunity and freedom and dreams for something bigger.

IN RANDY'S OWN WORDS My parents never went to college—my mom went to hairdressing school, and my dad went to the school of hard knocks.

So early on, college wasn't an aspiration for me. My plan, going into my freshman year of high school, was to become a coal miner. It wasn't until Ron's influence and the years

1970s Larry & Jean Lowe with Randy, Danny and Barb

of running cross country that I began to realize there was something more out there in the world for me. Eventually, I went from general classes to college prep and earned a personal development award for improvement from my freshman to senior years, as well as being inducted into the National Honor Society. I graduated in a much better position than those humble beginnings, in the top 10 percent of my class. Running really did make me a better student.

That culture was set by the team's older brothers, especially Tony, our top returning runner. Brent Marshall had been a great runner for us the year before, and after he graduated, Tony led the way forward.

Tony and P.J.—consistently our second-best runner—set an example, and demanded more from their teammates, in a way the previous year's seniors had not. And they were only *sophomores*.

It was the ultimate game of follow-the-leader, and P.J. was developing his own leadership skills and reinforcing Tony's example by pushing the pace during group training runs.

Their teammates didn't always love that! Some of them would have preferred a more casual pace. But P.J. was committed to maximizing our team's efforts, and if he set a fast pace, others were left following his lead. Caldwell's success came because the runners pushed each other to be better every single day in practice.

If someone slacked off or didn't give their best, P.J. wasn't afraid to speak up. He'd apply his leadership skills in Cub Scouts and 4-H, and he later became his senior class president and president of the National Honor Society.

IN P.J.'S OWN WORDS Doing what I did, being the vocal leader, wouldn't have mattered if we didn't have Tony, the physical leader. It left an opportunity for me to contribute in a way other than winning races.

With every ounce of my being, I just wanted to prove myself. I don't know why. I'm not sure if it was the validation, the competition, or just being a part of something greater than myself.

Some days I'd go out and try to really push Tony in practice, and 99 times out of 100, he pushed back. He usually pushed hard and would bury me. But that one time out of 100 when I'd get him, that raised the bar—for both of us.

Randy, another returning sophomore, contributed lots of heart to the team and was getting better and better with each run.

Thankfully, I didn't have trouble finding new runners in 1984—sixteen boys showed an interest in joining the team, and 10 wound up sticking with it through the season, including a number of actual siblings: the Lowes (Randy and Danny), the Norrises (P.J. and Brian), and the Fergusons (while Deuce was a senior, his younger brother Steve "Arnie" was a seventh grader coming up through the ranks).

That season's younger brothers, including another freshman, Stacy Huffman, helped to round out the core of Caldwell's team—a core that would run together for years to come. By following the lead of the older siblings, the incoming freshmen learned, through every practice, every run, and every meet, what it meant to pursue greatness and do things the right way.

Danny Lowe was small in size, but what he lacked in stature, he made up for with his work ethic and commitment. He and Randy were close—they were born only one year apart. Randy inspired Danny, setting an example of self-improvement and hard work. Randy had shed nearly two minutes off his times from the previous year. And Danny approached running with a similar intensity. Through Danny's workouts, it became obvious that he was going to be another freshman phenom like Tony.

Brian Norris, meanwhile, initially got into running because he got in trouble with his father—he got cut from his football team after ditching practice.

IN BRIAN'S OWN WORDS My brother was running track in junior high, and my dad saw he was enjoying it and having some success. I also think my dad thought it was another good sport and would keep me out of trouble.

So after I cut practice and I was grounded for a few weeks, my dad said he would "unground" me if I went out for track that year. That was all I needed to hear, and that spring, I started my running career as a seventh-grade track athlete.

I also coached the junior high track team, and when Brian came out for practice, I caught him and three of his friends cutting the course and not doing the full workout.

"That's not what I expect from members of this team," I told Brian and the other boys. "I want you to run laps around the school until I come back out."

I wanted to teach them to keep their commitments and give it their best without cutting corners. And since they weren't honest about their miles in on the road, running around the school gave them a chance to get their miles in while being watched more closely. I wanted to reinforce the reality that champions are made when no one is watching—and cutting corners would only leave them falling short of their goals.

By the time I returned, three of them had dropped out. But not Brian. He was still running. I'm thankful Brian stuck with it. He kept running and kept improving, and soon he was a sure thing.

He hadn't thought much about high school cross country until watching our state championship meet the previous year, but after seeing that race, he was hooked.

IN BRIAN'S OWN WORDS As a team, we were highly competitive and we wanted to win, but there's something that Ron drove within our team that made us special. It was more than just cross country. We all came from very unique homes and families—most of us being a part of single-parent households. Ron brought us all together, whether we knew it at the time or not.

Stacy Huffman, our other incoming freshman in 1984, was different than the rest of our runners—he was like a sleeping giant, ready to pounce. Stacy was really into the arts and also wrestled.

Wrestling is a lot like cross country in that it's both a team and individual sport. If you do your job, the team's going to benefit. That isn't the same in other team sports such as football, where you can miss a block and still have 10 other players out there helping you out, or if you're tired, the coach can send somebody in to take your spot. In wrestling and cross country, there is no relief—you have to go with the person who's out there and hope they get it done.

Coming into cross country, Stacy had the perfect build. He was tall and thin with long legs. He was also a tougher egg to crack. He had all the tools but lacked the knowledge about how to use those tools. Some athletes take a while to understand what it takes to get their desired results, but once they do, everything changes. Stacy was one of those athletes.

IN STACY'S OWN WORDS Starting out, I didn't know if I was going to make it. The first practice, I thought I was going to die on that first three-mile run. I think I walked most of it. But Ron persevered. He kept pushing and giving me more and more confidence, and as time went on, it became easier and easier. He made running as enjoyable as running could be.

Brian and Danny were friends with Stacy and convinced him to join the cross country team, along with J.D. Secrest and John Garrett. They all ran together over that summer, but Stacy really took to it. He eventually quit wrestling to focus solely on running, and the camaraderie between the new batch of runners grew throughout their freshman year.

Starting out, we didn't know what to expect from Stacy. Like a lot of the runners on our team, Stacy was enduring hardships in his home life. His father had died when Stacy was two years old, and his mother's new husband was abusive. Despite that, his mother raised five children while working a full-time job.

The crowd he hung out with before joining cross country were heading down the wrong road, too, getting into drugs and fights and trouble. It took Stacy some time to break free from all of that.

When Stacy was missing practice, his teammates would swing by his house and try to get him to join them. These runners weren't leaving one of their brothers behind. They needed him on the team—and they also wanted to keep him from getting in trouble for not coming to practice.

People who face tough times aren't always open about everything. They learn how to compartmentalize and hide parts of their life away from you. But cross country teams, like families, have rules and expectations to uphold. If someone missed practice, I'd make them participate in the JV race.

I did that with Stacy the first race of his high school career. He missed multiple practices, and I needed to send a message about commitment and being accountable to yourself and your teammates. He was held off of varsity that first race—he hadn't earned it. He ran the JV race instead and ended up winning, and that was his ticket back.

IN STACY'S OWN WORDS Ron would give you the silent treatment if he was upset about something. And of course the other guys followed suit. You know, that's the way we all did it: the silent treatment, which is a strong, strong thing to use against people you're close with. It gets the point across, and I felt horrible.

And then you talk to each other about the problem and address it "Hey, come on. You're kind of letting us down here." That helped.

The crop of promising young runners brought a lot of excitement to the coming season—but their meet performances displaced Deuce, a senior, out of the top five. As a senior, he would typically be our leading runner. But Deuce saw the situation for what it was, and instead of being bitter and moody and difficult, he stepped up as a leader for the younger runners.

IN DEUCE'S OWN WORDS In 1984, I started to feel as though running was not going to be something I would continue to do in college, especially when I looked at the new guard and saw how much talent the younger runners possessed. I continued to participate and made it through the 500 Mile Club, but I shifted my focus from runner to runner/coach. The '84 season is when that mentality kicked in, and I did as much as I could to support the other guys while participating as a runner and contributor on the team.

Deuce's leadership and support meant so much to the younger guys. It meant so much to me, too. And it provided a model for everyone else on selflessness and being a good teammate, of being good stewards and passing the torch to the next generation of runners.

Brian Norris reading to Coach Martin's kids: Heather and Chris

Having the runners all buy in made it easier, as the team's coach, to keep everyone on the same page. It also helped being able to relate to them. My own journey—including my father leaving and my parents getting divorced—helped me better understand what some of the runners faced, whether poverty or divorce or other struggles. Their difficulties reinforced the presence of team and brought us closer together.

Bev could also relate. Although she grew up in a two-parent household, her family was poor. A treat for Bev and her siblings was splitting a Chiclet.

It's difficult to put into words and not something I consciously thought about, it's just the way I felt. If someone needed help, I wanted to be there to help them, and running was the vehicle through which my wife and I had the opportunity to positively impact young people's lives.

KEY TO SUCCESS
CREATE A FAMILY ENVIRONMENT

We were able to create a family environment through team bonding. The runners were like family and loved being together.

My family's modest home was a gathering place for the runners. Our door was always open, and we all lived close to each other. The runners were looking for an escape, and we were glad to provide it. We would play cards or Intellivision, an old-school video game system with blocky 16-bit games and a handheld controller that looked like a TV remote. Or we would watch my beloved Detroit Tigers on TV.

Bev made homemade pizza and chocolate chip bar cookies for the runners. In turn, the runners played with and read to our young children, Christopher and Heather. These boys were family to us. There was never a time when it was inconvenient or a bother to have them over. At our house, they could feel welcome and have some fun together.

Top Chris and Heather Martin looking for the team.
Bottom Team playing cards at Coach Ron's house

IN P.J.'S OWN WORDS Caldwell offered very little from an entertainment perspective, and we couldn't afford to drive to Zanesville or Cambridge to go to restaurants, movies, or putt-putt, at least not very often. So much of our entertainment was eating spaghetti and pizza, playing cards, playing video games, watching movies, and just laughing and spending time together as a team.

The Martin home was a modest house—but it was a warm, happy home, and plenty big for all of us. It was our sanctuary, to some degree.

Those times at their house built a lot of trust and camaraderie—between Coach and us, and between us as teammates. We had a bond that is difficult to explain. We were all like brothers and friends as much as we were teammates. And Ron and Bev were as much parental figures as he was a coach.

IN STACY'S OWN WORDS Ron just had a way of making us better in all aspects. No matter the day of the week, if we were at Ron and Bev's house just hanging out, that day was the highlight of the week for me. I didn't have a strong family life myself, so Ron was like a stepdad to me. It allowed me to bond with my adopted family—my brothers. We really bonded there. It wasn't the competition that kept me involved. It was the brotherhood and the camaraderie. I didn't want to let the other guys down, so I kept running.

These runners spent so much time together. They would finish a full practice then play a game they called "Hollow Ball," which was like baseball but trickier. They played their game in the Hollow, an area behind P.J. and Brian's house that featured a downward slope into a field.

H-O-R-S-E, wiffle ball, you name it: if it was a competition, they were doing everything they could to finish their game until the streetlights came on.

KEY TO SUCCESS
BUILD A SUPPORT NETWORK

Family support for the team was very strong and critical to our success. This included attending meets, hosting team dinners, and financially supporting camps and national competitions.

Little Chris Martin with team members who are wearing plastic diaper covers as hats

Team dinners were another way to build rapport. The runners' parents took turns hosting team dinners in their homes each week. They typically served spaghetti and meatballs for carbohydrate loading on Thursday evenings before the weekend meets. Randy and Danny's parents owned a restaurant so we sometimes ate there as well. Those team dinners also helped me better connect with the runners' families.

It was rare to see so much rapport between teammates. Coaches can create an environment to help cultivate those bonds, but it's up to the runners themselves to carry those connections forward. Maybe their personalities clash, or their families don't get along, or one kid is jealous of another kid. Anything can shift that teammate connection.

But in 1984 and the years that followed, those bonds were unbreakable.

08.

SUCCESS DOESN'T COME EASY

The start of the 1984 season gave us a glimpse of the future: our core runners moving in unison like the pistons of a well-tuned engine.

Tony led the way, with P.J. right behind him. Our freshmen—Danny, Stacy, and Brian—were proving they were up for the challenge. It would be a lot of fun to watch this team over the coming years and dream about how successful they could become.

As a coach, it was important to recognize the runners reaching a new level.

That was the case at our first big race of the 1984 season, the Tiffin Cross Country Carnival, when P.J. was carrying himself with confidence during warmups—his legs quickly turned over.

"You look good," I told him. "No one can beat you."

I was right. No one—not even Tony—could beat him that day. For the first time in his competitive career, P.J. took medalist honors and beat out Tony, who finished in second place. Stacy placed fourth, Danny 10th, and Brent 12th.

It was necessary to have Tony face a challenge every now and again. He knew he couldn't slack off or slow down.

I kept the team's schedule busy near the start of the season ... and I regretted that later. Rest is important, and overtraining can certainly play a factor across a cross country season. Running more doesn't always mean running better. But that heartbreaking loss in the state championship meet the previous year was heavy on my mind. This team needed to stay hungry and keep challenging themselves.

IN P.J.'S OWN WORDS I'm still not sure what Ron saw that day, but he was right.

During the race, right after the creek we ran through, I started to pull away from Tony. I could hear Coach cheering me on, yelling, "Go get 'em!" When I finished the race in first place, I threw my arms up in victory as I crossed the finish. It was instinctual, maybe elation. I had never won a race before, let alone one as prestigious as the Tiffin Carnival. In any case, I should not have reacted like that. Tony didn't act like that when he won races. Coach Martin let me know it after the race: No showboating allowed.

Starting with Tiffin, we competed in four meets in 11 days, all of them easy victories. Ideally, we would compete just once a week, but we were under contract to run in two of the four meets. Looking back, racing that often didn't allow for enough rest and recovery.

Our underclassmen—Tony, P.J., Stacy, Danny, and Brian—were stepping up and driving our races. Even with a team of younger runners, we hadn't lost anything from the previous season. We hadn't really even been pressed in any of our early races, in part because the boys were putting up great numbers.

We were winning meets overwhelmingly. At the Brookville Invitational against 14 other teams in the Class A division, we scored just 21 points, placing six runners in the first nine finishers among a group of 93 runners. For the second time that season, we broke the record for largest margin of victory at a major invitational meet, this time 78 points.

The boys weren't being challenged enough, and I wanted them to take a crack at tougher competition, so I entered Caldwell into the larger-school division race for the Waterford Invitational. That race included Parkersburg South, the defending two-time West Virginia state champions,

Sophomore P.J. Norris

which would win another state championship that season. We were now facing off against the cream of the crop in the region.

Even that race—against larger schools—didn't stop us. Tony won his third consecutive race, followed close behind by P.J., Danny, Stacy, and Brian, and we remained undefeated on the season.

Maybe I'll revisit moving up again, I thought. I wanted to keep challenging the team.

The Malone College Invitational, a preeminent invitational that attracted top teams, was definitely a challenge. In 1984, it featured 25 teams from all corners of the state—including Cincinnati, Columbus, Cleveland and Toledo.[4]

How tough was the competition in this race? It was the only race the entire season in which Tony did not finish first or second; he crossed the finish line in fifth place, his worst finish of the season.

Be that as it may, it was pretty much business as usual, as the rest of the guys stepped up their game. P.J. finished eight seconds behind Tony for sixth

---

[4] Rusty Roberts, "Area Schools in AVAC Race," *The Daily Jeffersonian* (Cambridge, OH), September 20, 1984.

Senior Brent Sells

place, followed by Stacy (10th), Danny (12th), and Brian (17th). Our team of freshmen and sophomores finished with 50 points, beating second-place Avon, which scored 103. Our record remained unscathed at 88–0.

That race prepared us well for the following weekend at the Rio Grande Invitational, which included 16 other teams. We went down the night before, driving two hours and sleeping in the gym on wrestling mats.

The boys also got to visit their former teammate Brent Marshall, who was now running in college. It served as a reminder that cross country could open doors for them—and they could dream big.

The Rio Grande course was brutal, featuring steep hills with endless uphill turns.

Regaining his form, Tony crossed the finish line first. But it was a coming-out party for Danny, who finished third, besting P.J., and brought home a trophy.

We placed five runners in the top 10, with the day's best score of 27, topping second-place Cincinnati St. Bernard's 90 points.

We breezed through the regular season with a perfect 109-0 record and entered the postseason with confidence, easily winning the PVC League Championship.

It was state champions or bust. Our dream was within reach. The finish line was within focus.

But the heat was on as we entered the 1984 postseason. After coming so close in 1983 and laying waste to our competition during the regular season with a young, powerful team, we were the odds-on favorites to take home a state championship.

That put a bullseye on our backs. You never know what can happen, and we weren't taking anything for granted.

The Class A District Meet was held in October on the grounds of the Cambridge State Hospital, with a total of 10 teams participating. Tony, P.J., and Stacy swept the first three places as we defended the district title we had won the year prior. Danny and Brian came in seventh and ninth, aiding us in scoring 22 points, well ahead of Zanesville Rosecrans's 74. Randy and Brent put the exclamation point on the team's effort, placing 11th and 13th, respectively, finishing all seven runners in the top 13.

There was now just one meet remaining on the 1984 schedule: the 57th State Meet at the North Athletic Facility on the campus of Ohio State University. The day before the meet, *The Daily Jeffersonian* reported that in boys Class A, Caldwell "is considered the team to beat, with Dayton Christian, Stryker, and Cortland Maplewood the major challengers."[5]

Meanwhile, *Ohio Cross Country News* picked pesky Dayton Christian, the third-place team the year before, as "the heavy favorite." And in its listing of Class A teams headed to the state meet, it didn't even mention us. [6]

---

5 "Nearly 1,000 Runners Ready to Run at State," *The Daily Jeffersonian* (Cambridge, OH), October 26, 1984.

6 "Caldwell Team Ignored by Publication," *The Daily Jeffersonian* (Cambridge, OH), October 25, 1984

Homer Abrams and Randy

Combined with our two-point fall the prior year at state, this snub gave us an extra dose of motivation. It was a reminder that we still had something left to prove. We hadn't arrived quite yet.

Our team was also facing heavy hearts. The week of the state meet, Randy and Danny Lowe's paternal grandfather passed away. He was the first family member they had lost, and they struggled with processing a heavy grief. "Homer" was a US Navy veteran who had served in World War II. As the oldest of the grandkids, Randy and Danny were the closest to him, and they spent a lot of time together during their early years in Columbus.

He passed away after refusing cancer treatment. The grief and mourning from his death kept the boys out of town most of that week.

It's always tough when things take you out of focus and out of practice. But it was a reminder that even with the biggest race looming, there are always other elements at play—that life has a way of taking precedence and putting your priorities back in order.

We tried to put the sadness behind us on race day and focus on the task at hand.

This was our race. Someone from our school had even printed out a sign that ran the length of the interior of our school bus. It predicted a title and was more prideful than our typical nature. But we left it hanging.

After all, we were going to win, right?

The state meet was held on an unseasonably warm late-October day—80 degrees with partly cloudy skies. The heat played a major factor in the day's events. It likely didn't help that the guys were wearing the black warm-ups we had been using since 1982. We only had seven sets of them (plus two for my assistant coach and me). The budget was so small that as the team grew, younger runners had to wear the girls' red warm-ups.

IN DANNY'S OWN WORDS I remember warming up in our black silks, which were hot because black absorbs heat. It was pretty hot, and I was sweating profusely because I was nervous. It was my first time at state meet. And I remember at the start, taking off like I didn't know what I was doing.

L to R P.J., Danny, and Brian warming up

L to R Brent, Danny, Tony and P.J. stretching

We prepared as we always did, running the course ahead of time to make sure there were no surprises. I wanted to give my freshmen runners a chance to experience each twist and turn of the course.

The race we'd spent a full year preparing for was upon us.

IN STACY'S OWN WORDS I kept reminding myself to go out easy ... go out easy ... . Everyone was positioned in their respective boxes ... . The starter walked to the middle of the field, raised the flag ... BANG! I could feel the elbows hitting my arms, chest, and ribs. Spikes to the shins, calves, and knees. Heavy breathing everywhere and pounding of what sounded like hundreds of feet hitting the sod all while hearing nothing else outside the race itself.

I was positioned in the fields in the early part of the race and shouted encouragement to the runners. They were running great in the early going.

As usual, Tony was a rocket. He had been gunning to win this race for a full year.

At the two-mile mark, our runners were still going strong, with Tony out in front and our three freshmen—Danny, Brian, and Stacy—in good position. Danny was positioned in the top 10 ahead of P.J.

As the runners passed me, I sprinted—over hills, on a trail, and around people, with my clipboard under my arm—to a spot near the finish line so I could watch the runners finish.

The biggest runners show up at the biggest moments, and that was Tony. He chugged forward, his legs a speeding locomotive, and crossed the finish line a full seven seconds ahead of any of the other 83 runners.

IN TONY'S OWN WORDS Winning my first state title at the 1984 cross country state meet is one of my fondest

Sophomore Tony Carna wins the State Championship

> memories. Crossing the finish line to capture the state title
> is etched into my mind. It's a very vivid memory and I can
> still close my eyes and see my foot hitting the line. I did it!

As the race played out, I felt confident in our chances.

The championship was within reach.

The 12th- through 15th-place finishers were all from Caldwell and Dayton Christian: Dave Richards and Jeff Fear finished 12th and 13th for the Warriors, while P.J. and Stacy were 14th and 15th for Caldwell. This left us trailing by just a single point, with the final two scorers for each team yet to finish.

But what about Danny? Our freshman phenom had been running a great race and should have finished by now.

A few hundred yards from the finish line, Danny started to fade.

Finishing in 18th place was Brian, with Mike Marriott of the Warriors a second behind in 20th place. With just one more scorer for each team yet to cross the finish line, we had pulled ahead by one point, 48–49.

Had Danny been able to hold onto that position, we would have been assured the victory, but the heat caught up with him. Danny became dehydrated.

He kept slowing down and began swaying side to side as others passed him.

> IN DANNY'S OWN WORD It was like I was looking through a
> tunnel at the finish line. I could see the finish line focused, but
> everything else was a blur. And as I kept getting closer and
> closer, I kept losing more and more control of my body and
> eventually almost started running backwards at the end, two
> steps forward, one step back, two steps forward, one step back.
>
> I could hear everything, but my sight started to go. And I
> knew something was going on because I couldn't see. And I
> couldn't control my body. The only thing I kept repeating in
> my mind was "finish, finish, finish." At the 100, it was just "get
> to the finish line, get to the finish line." And I could see people
> passing me, but they were blurs. They weren't even in focus.

Top Danny Fading
Bottom Danny struggling to finish

I was worried about the state championship. But I was more worried about my runner.

As the *Daily Jeffersonian* reported it: "Twenty yards before the finish, Lowe went into a stagger barely managing to keep his balance. Courageously, he finished the race, but not before 24 runners had passed him."[7] He stumbled across the finish line in 47th place. The heat was a factor for another dozen runners that day, with a few being taken to the nearby hospital, although none were admitted.

Danny received medical care after crossing the finish line. The good Lord was looking over him that day. His primary care physician, Dr. Fred Cox, was a spectator and tended to Danny as soon as he finished.

Danny's parents were in the crowd, and his father, Larry, had to be restrained from grabbing his son, as it would have caused a disqualification if anyone touched him before he crossed the finish line.

With Danny fading so far behind, Sells ended up being our fifth man, coming in at 32nd place. However, Tim Combs of Dayton Christian was two seconds ahead of him, placing 30th.

The officials tabulated the score.

Caldwell had 80 points.

Dayton Christian scored 79.

Our hopes for a state title were thwarted for the second straight year, by an even smaller margin.

Losing by one or two points in cross country is tight. It's not football or basketball, where comebacks come down to time and possession. It's like losing a game on a last-second fluke play in which one of your leading scorers has to leave the game and you suddenly aren't able to count any of their points toward the team's score. It's just hard to even describe—especially when we thought we were going to win by 30.

It was little consolation to know that with a record of 261–2 over the last two seasons, the Caldwell team had posted the best record in the state. We didn't have a state championship to show for it.

We sulked and hung our heads.

---

7 Ibid.

1984 State Meet Runners Up – Team on Podium

IN TONY'S OWN WORDS That was the roughest bus ride home. We just missed and lost. We were so down. We thought, *How could this be?*

IN STACY'S OWN WORDS After the race, someone walked by and saw the sign hanging inside our bus and started ribbing us a little bit: "Ah, it didn't happen." We missed it by that much.

I talked to the guys, individually and together, motivating and consoling them. My immediate, most pressing need was to let Danny know this wasn't his fault. We didn't lose because of him—in fact, he was a major reason we made it as far as we did. His body gave out at the most inopportune time. But there was nothing, from a preparation or desire or determination standpoint, that he could have done differently.

1984 Team: Front L To R Brian Norris, J.D. Secrest, Stacy Huffman, Arnie Ferguson **Back L To R** Assistant Coach Dugan Hill, Randy Lowe, Danny Lowe, Deuce Ferguson, Brent Sells, John Garrett, Tony Carna, P.J. Norris, Head Coach Ron Martin

IN DANNY'S OWN WORDS It was the most disappointing moment for me. I felt like I lost it all for us, like I had let everyone else down.

This hurt for me, too. But there was always a lesson. I wanted to motivate runners like Brian. He'd finished a respectable 18th place, but I didn't want him to rest on that and be content.

I took him aside. "Hey, great race," I told him, "but I really thought you would have done better. You're a big-race guy. You love competition. I was just expecting that you were going to go out there and have an incredible race." I knew he had a strong race, but I also knew this would drive him even more.

IN BRIAN'S OWN WORDS I thought to myself, *I had a good race*, but Ron's words really stuck with me in the offseason.

Ron always had a way of getting to people and getting them to think about what they have and have not accomplished. That was one of the bigger turning points in my career, and I'm fortunate it came early for me.

The bus ride home was quiet and somber. I spoke to the team from the heart. I was so proud of them—prouder than they'd ever know—but we had fallen short again.

"Guys, a lot of teams would love to be second in the state," I told the team. But we weren't one of those teams. They all knew it, too.

We had done *everything* we could and still lost. We needed to do something drastic.

In order to win, something had to change.

PART IV
BREAKING THROUGH: 1985

09.

THE DECISION

Shell-shocked.

Haunted.

Cursed.

There were so many feelings running through my mind after we lost in heartbreak, again, at the state championship meet.

Would we ever break through?

How was this even possible?

In the past two seasons, we'd lost twice—by a total of three points. In terms of race time, the margin of error was about as big as the time it takes you to read this sentence.

Or this one.

Or maybe this one.

In order to learn from our past mistakes, we had to look at the failures and letdowns from the 1984 season.

The runners' effort wasn't the problem. No kid works as hard as our runners did and enters a race with the thoughts of running poorly or a feeling of indifference—they all wanted to race well. They all wanted to win, and they did everything I asked of them.

While I felt responsible for the way the team performed, I didn't think my training approach was an issue—if it had been, we would have lost at other points during the 1983 and 1984 seasons. Our approach was based on years of adjustments and refinements and input from the best minds in the running world.

My mind ran through all of the possible reasons why we'd come up short. Race tactics? No... Mental preparation? Probably not...

Competition?

As I often told my runners, "We can only control how we compete!" But maybe there was something I could do to improve the level of our competition. During the 1984 season, we dominated our opponents, with an average score of 33—meaning our fifth runner finished somewhere in 10th to 15th place. Throughout the season, we coasted to victory without too many real challenges against similarly sized schools, leaving us ill-equipped to handle the higher level of competition in the state meet.

As I talked to other coaches and people I trusted that offseason, and after lots of soul searching, I came to the conclusion that we were not prepared mentally for the state meet.

Simply put, we weren't facing competitive enough teams to properly prepare for the state meet. We were untested during the regular season, and the team had to have more pressure, more grit, and maybe even understand what it is like to lose before the big meet.

Scheduling the same races against the same teams for the upcoming season could bring about the same result.

Maybe we could run against better competition, just as we'd done in 1984 at the Waterford Invitational. We held our own in that race.

We would never know how good we truly were if we stayed complacent and continued racing small or midsize schools. I wanted to put these runners to the test. We needed to do *something* to get over the hump—and maybe this was it.

Teams typically try to move down to pad their stats or shift classes based on their student population. My thought was to race the toughest competition, get beat, and humble ourselves a little bit.

A little bit was the key. If the move up was too challenging and we lost soundly, if we were clearly not ready to face the big schools, the experiment could crush our runners' confidence.

Through this experiment, I thought our athletes would finish further down in the pack—somewhere around 20th or 30th—which was closer to the type of finish we could expect from the state meet. If they were better equipped to face challenging runners, the state championship meet would be less stressful, and there would be less emphasis on that one meet.

We had the talent, heading into 1985, to give this a go. With Tony Carna, P.J. Norris and his brother Brian, the Lowe brothers Randy and Danny, and Stacy Huffman all returning and contributing and fighting for a top-five finish, we had a very good and experienced group of runners heading into the 1985 season.

When I ran my idea past other coaches, they looked at me like I was crazy.

"Which race would you try this?" they asked.

"Every race," I said.

They cautioned me to take it slow. To not jump in with both feet. To try it with some early meets then decide if we should move down to AA or even stay in Class A.

But my mind was made up.

For me, it was all or nothing; I have always been all in. We were always asking our kids to get out of their comfort zone, so I had to practice what I preached.

It wasn't enough just to think it through and make my decision—I had to get state officials to sign off on my plan. So in the spring of 1985 I called the Ohio High School Athletic Association. They didn't have a commissioner for cross country at the time, and the workers didn't really know who should field my call. This was an unusual request.

"Why do you want to do that? Are you trying to punish your team?" they asked.

No, I need them to be challenged, and I need to see how they react to that challenge.

"Okay..."

I could tell they weren't convinced. They didn't understand.

Someone found the cross country bylaws and scanned them, line by line, as I waited with my ear to the phone in anticipation.

One line in a dusty document could derail my entire plan. But I was committed to take this as far as I needed to get it approved. I couldn't bear to see us lose the state championship again by mere moments, and neither could the runners.

After what felt like an eternity, the OHSAA staffer got back on the phone.

"There is nothing in the rules stating that a smaller team can't move up to the larger divisions in regular season play, but it's entirely up to the meet managers of each individual invitational," they told me. "However, in postseason play, the schools must compete in their own division."

I planned to move up in every single meet we could.

I could feel the fury and frustration simmering as I wrote my letter to the boys that summer alerting them to my change of plans. My "1985 Team Goals" included some new and very ambitious objectives for the coming season:

1985 Team Goals

I. Live Up To The #1 Ranking which has been given to the Caldwell Cross Country Program. As far as I'm concerned being ranked #1 means nothing unless you can produce when you need to. Caldwell should have 3 or 4 State Titles and we only have one. What does that tell you?????? Let's begin a dynasty.

II. I want to be the Best Team In The Whole State We are going to move up to the big school division whenever we can. I want to race the best and I want to beat the best.

III. As far as individual places in big meets, I'll let you fill out your own goal sheet. I would like to have 5 guys in the top 10 and all 7 in the top 20. This may vary when we move up to a bigger division but not much. (5 in the top 15, 7 in top 30)

IV. Win P.V.C. (I want the Top 6 finishers)

V. Win Districts + Regionals with less than 25 points

VI. Win State with less than 30 points

VII. Have 5 All-Ohioans

VIII. Most of all I want you guys to be impressive in every big meet you're in and enjoy your victories. Keep everything in order and use your heads when things start falling into place for you.

These goals were overly ambitious, bordering on unattainable. Our best score at the state meet in the last two seasons had been 80 points. Winning state with less than 30 points was almost unthinkable—it would require us to utterly dominate the field. We also set out to have five All-Ohioans on the team, which would mean, based on updated rules for 1985, that Caldwell would have to have five runners finish among the first 12 at the state meet.

My thinking? We needed to do something unthinkable and revolutionary in order to break through.

KEY TO SUCCESS
ATHLETE BUY-IN
The athletes were all in! They bought into
everything we were doing.

I didn't doubt or question my decision for us to face bigger schools, but in order for this to work, Caldwell's runners would have to buy in and believe. This group of teenagers would have to work harder and push each other and demand even more out of themselves and each other.

The runners had mixed feelings about moving up. Facing bigger schools would make it that much harder for us to win meets and for the runners to receive individual accolades. Moving up could cost them awards and attention.

IN RANDY'S OWN WORDS The pivotal point was when Ron told us we were no longer messing around here. We weren't going to be second place anymore. Those days were over. When I received that letter notifying us that we were going to begin competing against the bigger schools starting in 1985, I knew it was time for us to hunker down and get ready. As a team, as brothers, we were ready to get together and do it right.

IN TONY'S OWN WORDS Hearing the news about leveling up was sobering, especially when a group of goofballs like us finally got quiet and got serious about the challenge to come. Nobody objected. Nobody wanted to back down from the competition. We wanted to get out there with the heavyweights and see what we were made of.

But even if there were some mixed feelings, the runners still had something to prove, just as I did. They wanted to be great. Here was the chance to see how good we truly were.

The challenge was set. New, fierce foes awaited.

Now it was time to get to work.

10.

THE BOYS OF SUMMER

My teams had always worked hard in the offseason.

But that summer of 1985, the team reached a new gear. The boys were running with purpose.

The decision to move up to run against bigger schools lit a fire for them—they had something to prove.

Moving up took us out of our comfort zones. We were familiar with the Class A schools and knew the teams and runners to watch, but thinking about running against the best teams from every corner of the state—teams like Mentor, from the Cleveland area; Westerville North, a suburb of Columbus; and Cincinnati Elder and St. Xavier out of Cincinnati—was daunting.

These were the big schools. Top of the top.

And here we were, a bunch of kids from a town most people in the state had never heard of.

In order to compete and hold our own, we needed to put in a bunch of miles and build our base in preparation for the season.

And our core of six runners—Tony, P.J., Brian, Danny, Stacy, and Randy—were hitting the pavement every day at 9 a.m. and 7 p.m.

Nobody missed.

Nobody cut corners.

No complaints.

No excuses.

With each run, they were maturing and coming into their own. They had experience and talent, and their runs were becoming more professional and businesslike. Each runner held his fellow runners accountable, and it was a battle every day to see who was going to run better.

Tony was Mr. Consistency, always at the front of the pack. On certain days, P.J. was feeling good and running well, and he would start to push things a little bit. Other days it was Brian or Danny.

For an eight-mile run, the runners would be bunched together for the first four miles, then about halfway in, there would be a little separation. Two or three guys would take the lead and another two or three guys would start to drop back.

But the runners in the front weren't leaving their teammates behind. "Come on, guys," P.J. and the others at the front would yell. "Stick with us. Stay with the lead pack." They were pulling and motivating their teammates to stay with that lead pack as long as they could.

IN RANDY'S OWN WORDS We took things a little more serious that summer, and not the quantity of miles, but the quality. We pushed each other. That wasn't a normal 500 Club. We weren't cutting corners or laying in the ditch and trying to get out of mileage. Of course, you always had P.J. pushing the pace. That's what he's famous for. But we felt like we pushed ourselves a little more that summer.

As a coach, I loved to see that camaraderie. Cross country can be a very jealous sport—runners can aim to be the best on their team at the expense of their teammates—but that was never the case with this team. They wanted themselves *and* their teammates to run their best.

That effort and determination shone through the most with Randy, who made incremental progress throughout his first two seasons running cross country. By 1985, Randy had hit a growth spurt—he was no longer the scrawny, small kid who had started running with us two years earlier.

Danny and Tony stretching before a summer run

Shaving a minute here and a minute there off his times transformed him into a true contributor, someone who was gunning for our top five in any race.

Randy's progress gave us depth and flexibility. If someone couldn't finish the race or got hurt, we could still win with Randy's score. We didn't have that flexibility in seasons past.

It was inspiring seeing these kids working so hard and devoting their summer to the team. They deserved a chance to showcase their talents—and that opportunity came during the last weekend of July, with the Athletic Congress (TAC) National Junior Olympics track and field meet at the University of Washington in Seattle.

I wanted our runners to think big.

Six athletes represented our small school at this prestigious event.

Paying for the trip wasn't cheap. It cost more money than any of us could afford—about $2,000 total—but the community chipped in. The runners held a 12-hour relay—a brutal, all-night ordeal that lasted from

1985 Postcard from Seattle, Washington

7 p.m. until 7 a.m.—and appealed to the Noble County commissioners to help cover the expenses.

For the relays, individuals and businesses sponsored the runners by kicking in 50 cents or a dollar per mile. The generosity of community members made trips like the one to Seattle—and the following season, to Lincoln, Nebraska—possible.

As we'd come to expect, Tony got the guys started by running in the 5,000-meter (3.1-mile) race as one of six runners in a pack, bunched together and trading the lead back and forth. He had been doing a lot of distance training, and with 600 meters to go, he made his move.

Another runner nipped at his heels.

The race came down to the final 40 yards, with Tony and the runner jockeying for the finish. In a photo finish, Tony won on a lean by two-tenths of a second! Not only did he win the race for the 15–16 age group, but he set a new national meet record time of 15:12.77, about a second-and-a-half faster than the previous record.

Or so we thought.

Junior Olympics '85

© 1984 HERBERT PARSONS

1985
TAC/USA
JUNIOR OLYMPIC
NATIONAL CHAMPIONSHIPS
UNIVERSITY OF WASHINGTON · Seattle, Wa

THE ATHLETICS
CONGRESS
TAC
USA

July 24 & 25 ATHLONS
July 24-28 TRACK & FIELD
July 28   10K ROAD RACE

1985 TAC/Junior Olympics Program

The race officials issued a red flag, suggesting that he made illegal contact with other runners. They talked back and forth for what felt like forever—15, 20, 45 minutes—discussing whether Tony should be disqualified.

> IN TONY'S OWN WORDS There was this open debate about whether or not I was fouling people during the course of the race. But the funny thing is, I don't remember seeing a red flag during the race. And I don't remember an official saying a word to me.
>
> It was so heavy. Did I really just come here and run the race of my life, only to have it taken away for normal bumping?

Eventually, the officials ruled in Tony's favor, and the victory and record were secured.

The next day, four of the boys competed in the 10,000-meter (6.2-mile) run. Tony led once again, finishing third. It was a pretty remarkable achievement, since he had won the 5,000-meter event the day before.

Tony—who, as a freshman, was all lungs and no legs and needed to build up his strength—was now learning how to finish races and kick his talent into a new gear.

> IN TONY'S OWN WORDS It was very warm the morning we ran the 10,000, and I had just run the race of my life the evening before. I did the best that I could, but I wasn't able to stay with the leaders.

Tony finished in third place, Brian was fourth, and Danny was fifth for the 15–16-year-olds, while Randy set a personal record. Stacy finished in a respectable 12th place in the 2,000-meter steeplechase—a feat made all the more impressive by the fact that he was a newcomer to the event.

To top it off, another Caldwell student, Dail Harper, competed in the shot put event. The previous year, Harper had participated in the TAC National Junior Olympics and won the event for the 15–16 age group. This time, he was in the 17–18 age group and finished second, good enough to earn him All-America recognition, his second in as many years.

What an incredible performance by a group of athletes from one of the smallest schools at the event! Caldwell's cross country season was still about a month away, but the team's top runners were primed and ready to go.

For the runners, the trip was meaningful for lots of reasons. It helped them see results of their hard work and helped them believe in something bigger for the team. Maybe moving up to face bigger schools wasn't such a bad idea, after all.

The trip allowed them to connect with other athletes from all over the country and compare notes. It was also the first time many of them saw so much of the country. It was a chance for them to step out of our corner of Ohio and see the greater world.

IN DANNY'S OWN WORDS It really spurred me into traveling later in life. I went back to Seattle last year and visited the track we ran on, and I climbed Mount Rainier because we didn't go there as a team. Part of the reason why I travel is because we traveled when we were in high school.

Considering our previous state title near misses and the fact that all of our top runners were returning, Caldwell started generating lots of hype. Ahead of the 1985 season, Ed Chay wrote in *Ohio Cross Country News* that "Ron Martin may have the best team in the state regardless of class."[8]

May have. People still didn't know what to make of our team. But given our goal of running against bigger schools, we would soon know for sure whether his assessment was valid.

Tony, now a junior, was our undisputed leader.

Our number two was P.J., also a junior and a fine long-distance runner in his own right.

---

8 Ed Chay, "Caldwell May Be the Best Team in Ohio," *Ohio Cross Country News,* Sept. 5, 1985.

They were followed by Danny, Stacy, Brian and Randy, as well as freshman newcomer Chris Fleming. This was indeed a young team, yet one loaded with experience and accomplishments—and looking to do even better.

The team's dedication only deepened after we returned from Seattle. That dedication was reflected in Brian's perseverance following an injury.

Brian was dealing with jet lag from our trip home. After oversleeping, he was hurrying on his bike down a huge hill between his house and the school, where we were gathered for practice. Heading downhill, his spikes got caught in the bike's front tire and he face planted on the asphalt and loose gravel.

He lost three teeth and had road rash on his face and shoulder, and he spent the night at the hospital. The next day he had emergency dental work done.

After spending some time with his grandmother and aunt in Michigan, he was back to work, competing in practice every day.

IN BRIAN'S OWN WORDS This was the first couple of weeks of August, so I knew how important this training was for the season. I ran every day with a missing front tooth and one tooth on each side grinded down to a stub until my temporary bridge could make it in.

As a team, we'd taken some tumbles. But this group kept responding. As the last gasp of summer gave way for the fall season, Caldwell's cross country team was ready to face its greatest challenge yet.

11.

TO BE THE BEST, YOU HAVE TO BEAT THE BEST

We were full of adrenaline and butterflies as our bus pulled up at Hedges-Boyer Park in Tiffin, home of the Tiffin Cross County Carnival.

Our team had raced—and won—this event the previous two years, but in the smaller-school category. This time, we would be competing against 19 much larger schools, and in the "fast" race, at that. (The field for the bigger-school division was split into two because it was so large). This race would show us if we belonged or if we were pretenders.

Running at Tiffin against the larger schools was like putting on 3D glasses. It forced you to see things in a new way. Details you hadn't previously recognized popped out at you.

Class divisions—big and small, haves and have-nots—were obvious as we arrived. The massive schools had multiple buses, team tents, brand-new uniforms and spikes, and parents bringing coolers of food and drinks. We arrived in our rickety bus, with no tent and no snacks.

Teams like Cincinnati Elder and Cleveland St. Ignatius, with 60 or 90 runners, were warming up in big circles, with people in the middle calling out regimented drills. There was an intimidation factor at play.

IN BRIAN'S OWN WORDS It was the first real test. Even though I had been to many meets before this one, I never really paid attention to the big schools. However, when you are going to race against them, you notice different things. And the one vivid memory I had was arriving early in the morning on our bus and seeing our 10 or 12 guys come off our bus and then seeing 60, 70, 80-plus runners come off the big school buses. Deep down, I knew each team only ran seven guys, but it was intimidating to see.

No matter. We just had to block all of that out. As I often told the team, "Take care of *your* business. Focus on what you can control. Everything else will take care of itself."

Caldwell's team members stretched, jogged the course, stretched some more, got our numbers affixed to our singlets, and did our prerace build-ups at the starting line. We focused on the task at hand and tried to calm our nerves.

In the lead-up to the race, P.J. was doing run-outs at the starting line to get his legs ready when a runner from another school approached him.

"What are you guys doing here? We're going to smoke you. Don't you know you're too small to win?" the runner asked.

P.J. came back to the team, and when we huddled up at the line, he told the other guys what the runner said. Too small to win, huh? That comment stuck with us.

IN P.J.'S OWN WORDS When I told the guys about the runner's comment, there was this feeling of, *All right, let's go.* It focused the team and helped us block out the distractions and noise.

As if that wasn't enough, the heat that day was intense. As Barry Peters of the Tiffin *Advertiser-Tribune* wrote, "[The] weather was the talk of Hedges-Boyer Park and many coaches wouldn't let their runners compete because of the heat."[9]

---

9 Barry Peters. "Heat's turned on at Columbian Carnival," *The Advertiser-Tribune*, (Tiffin, OH), Sept. 8, 1985.

While it may have been the Saturday after Labor Day, the weather was more akin to the Fourth of July. The temperature was above 90 degrees for most of the event, topping out at 92, with humidity as thick as fog.

The race was the exact type of challenge I had hoped for—the perfect test of all our preparation and a way for us to see how our runners matched up against many of the state's best schools.

The way the race was set up was daunting. The runners had to go over a road at the start, and all you heard was the clack-clack-clack of their spikes. Signs and obstacles funneled the runners and forced them to stay alert.

IN BRIAN'S OWN WORDS When we were on the starting line doing our run out warm-ups, I remember being more nervous than I ever had been. One of the teams in the box next to us said, "Hey, wasn't the small kids' division earlier in the day?" There was no doubt many other teams thought we were out of our league and we did not belong. My nervousness quickly turned to insecurity and uncertainty. But when that gun went off, the adrenaline kicked in and we fell into our routine.

IN P.J.'S OWN WORDS Standing on the starting line at Tiffin in '85 was probably the most nervous I ever was in my life—and the most adrenaline I felt at the start of a race. When you crossed over the road, there were probably 2,000 spikes clacking, but it sounded like 10,000 spikes. Usually in a race, you're spread out, but because we were all crossing at the same time, there was so much excitement.

Between the click-clack of spikes, the heat, and the challenge we faced against all these larger schools, I felt that excitement, too.

The race felt like it was being run in slow motion. Everyone's time was a little bit slower due to the conditions, but as I stood near the end of the course waiting for the runners to come up a crest before they finished on a half-mile loop, the seconds and moments seemed to hang in place.

Junior Tony Carna

I believed in this team more than any group of people I've encountered in my life.

But maybe I'd pushed them too hard. Maybe they wouldn't rise to this challenge. Maybe this was too much to ask. Maybe I was being foolish about everything.

The questions and doubts swirled until Caldwell's runners started to come up the hill, one after another.

Tony was the first runner up the crest on his way to a first-place medal, which gave me hope. The other runners weren't far behind. P.J. managed a third-place finish, while Stacy came in eighth, Brian finished 18th, and Randy was 36th. As each of them came up the hill, I shouted encouragement to motivate them to finish strong.

"This is the finish! He will pass you! Use that kick you have!" I yelled to Stacy.

IN STACY'S OWN WORDS Ron was saying the right things, and I just remember taking off and that guy was nowhere near me at the end of the race. Ron knew what to say.

When Randy's brother Danny was unable to finish the race due to the heat, Randy's time and finishing position were more than enough to secure the team win for Caldwell. Randy, who was our team's fifth finisher, beat not only every other team's number five runner but also all of the other number four runners. It was a reminder of how much depth this team had, even compared to a season earlier when we didn't have an answer to Danny's heat exhaustion in the state championship meet. Now, after losing Danny, one of our better runners, we had enough depth to win against some of the state's biggest, best teams.

In the end, we earned a score of 66, easily bettering a pair of Class AAA state powerhouses, second-place Shelby High School and its 129 points and third-place Cincinnati Elder with 138 points.

> IN P.J.'S OWN WORDS Until that year's Tiffin race,
> I didn't know if we belonged. And I think that was one
> of the defining moments of our entire high school career.

In the Tiffin race, Caldwell defeated about half of the leading Class AAA teams that would run in that year's state meet, including no. 2 Shelby, no. 3 Toledo St. Francis de Sales, and no. 7 Cincinnati Elder. Our goal of being the best cross country team in Ohio was off to a promising start. We believed that we belonged, no matter how big the competition.

Randy's development as a runner, and the depth it provided us, transformed us from a solid but beatable team into a juggernaut. Not many teams could lose a top runner against premiere competition and still win. But that's exactly what happened at Tiffin.

Any cross country team is only as good as its fifth or sixth runner. It's common to come across teams with two or three good runners but without any depth—and their team scores suffer due to their fourth and fifth runners.

With Randy's emergence, we became a complete team.

Our team was so disciplined, with so much camaraderie, that we effectively used races as workouts, focusing on running our best race instead of trying to run against someone else.

We faced out-of-state competition when we traveled to Parkersburg, West Virginia to race against six other teams in the River City Runners Invitational at Parkersburg Community College. This time, the weather couldn't be nicer for a race, with a high in the mid-60s. We took the first six places before an awestruck crowd—or, as one reporter described it, "Caldwell, Caldwell, Caldwell, Caldwell, Caldwell, Caldwell."[10]

As usual, Tony finished first, followed by P.J. Danny, Brian, Stacy, and Randy. That gave us a perfect score of 15 points. Parkersburg, one of the better teams in West Virginia, was second with 68 points.

There was an interesting "race within the race" taking place at this event. George Angelos, one of West Virginia's all-time great distance runners, was running for Parkersburg High School. His strategy for this race was to run with Tony as long as possible in an effort to gain a top finish. That strategy worked for a while, but sticking with Tony proved to be too much for him. In the end, George finished a very respectable seventh place behind our guys.

At the next race, the Dover Invitational in northeastern Ohio, we failed to score another perfect 15, but we came pretty close, finishing with 20 points to easily defeat second-place New Philadelphia and its 50 points.

"You guys were about the only team that could beat us," New Philadelphia runner Frank Fry recalled years later. "We always were gunning for ya, that's for sure."

New Philadelphia's Matt Whitis agreed.

"We knew you were coming but didn't know you were in our division until close to race time, when our coach told us," he said. "I had that 'uh-oh' moment as we tried to quickly wrap our brains around it before going to the line. You guys commanded respect wherever you went."

Finishing first as he had done in every previous race, Tony led from the outset at a blistering pace over a 3.1-mile course that featured, as one newspaper put it, "Two hills most people have trouble walking up." P.J. placed second, with Danny just three seconds behind him in third. Brian placed fifth, Stacy ninth, and Randy 11th, just three seconds behind Stacy.

---

10 Jett, Carroll, "Caldwell Captures RCR Invitational..." *The Parkersburg News*, Sept. 11, 1985.

Tony Carna finishing hard

The race had a dangerous hill that was very steep and had a turn at the bottom. Steep uphills can be navigated easily, but a steep downhill with a turn is a recipe for a twisted ankle or lower-leg injury. We didn't go back to that race again because of the dangerous conditions.

Something else happened after the race that worried me, too. People were looking at the stats for the top 10 finishers, including a couple of parents of another team. Someone made a comment about how good Caldwell was due to our low score, and Randy made a concerning comment. "I finished 11th overall, and I did not even make the top 5 for my team," he said.

The comment was borne out of frustration and personal pride. Running on a successful team requires you to put your ego aside. Randy felt like he wasn't getting the individual respect that he deserved—that he didn't matter as much because we had so many other good runners.

But he did matter. He brought hustle to the team and helped get the best out of his teammates.

I pulled the team onto the bus to talk to them. I wanted us to be confident but not cocky. They needed to keep their egos in check. We were good—really, really good. But we hadn't won the state meet yet. And this group, if it kept a level head and stayed focused on the team, had a chance to be great.

> IN RANDY'S OWN WORDS I didn't mean anything by my comment, I was just frustrated to be sixth man on this great team, 11th overall, and not even score. Ron told us 100 times, "Be confident, not cocky," and it was a good teachable moment for all of us to keep us all in check.

Switching our schedule to focus on bigger meets against large-school opponents had ripple effects I hadn't considered—namely, it was a culture shock because it reinforced the economic realities about Caldwell.

Our typical Class A opponents faced similar financial realities as Caldwell. That wasn't true about some of the bigger schools—they had big budgets and deep-pocketed sponsors, and as a result, they had new buses and tents and outfits. By Caldwell standards, the members of the team were middle class. But by outside standards, most of them were lower middle class.

It was inexpensive to live in Caldwell, and most of the runners didn't have much money. Getting an extra five dollars from their parents was a big thing. Most of them didn't have cars—and they didn't have much use for them.

Thankfully, with cross country there wasn't much gear to buy. You really just needed a reliable pair of shoes. But even those could be expensive for the team members. Shoes were often passed down from one sibling to the next, and sometimes from one runner to another.

> IN P.J.'S OWN WORDS I remember going into a mall in West Virginia, and I needed a pair of shoes to run. I took dad into the Foot Locker, and there were a pair of Nike sneakers with the waffle sole on it, and I want

to say they were $38. He looked at me with a worried look. "It's going to be 40 bucks for this pair of shoes?!" That was a lot for us. It was not easy to come by good equipment—we simply didn't have the money.

Running provided team members an affordable way to round out their wardrobe. They would often get T-shirts from running in 5Ks, and they wore those shirts *everywhere*. Even as their coach, I had a practice shirt I wore every day, and at the end of the month, I would take it home and wash it.

IN P.J.'S OWN WORDS Runners at other schools would be wearing nice shoes, and it made me feel like they've gotta be good—their parents spent a lot of money on those shoes. But I didn't care if we were too small, too Appalachian, too poor. None of that mattered when the race began. When the gun went off, it was an even playing field. Everything else was just noise, a distraction from the end goal.

Crisscrossing the state in our team bus bonded our team more tightly and also brought out their mischievous side.

The runners played card games and told stories and cracked jokes on the long bus rides. That was the era of the boombox, and they would often play music and fight over AC/DC or Run-DMC or Prince. They tried to sing along, too, which was a catastrophe.

Sometimes we caught some shut-eye. Other times we tossed and turned or just closed our eyes.

On the rides back to Caldwell, we talked about the meet and which of Caldwell's runners moved up or moved back in position after the mile mark.

If we stopped at McDonald's—that was a big deal for us—the team had a bad habit of using paper from the straws to fire spit wads at the bus driver until the inside of the windshield looked like it had snowed. One time, while I was stretched out trying to rest on the front two seats, the guys were horsing around. "Guys, knock it off," I told them. As I laid back down, a napkin full of chocolate milkshake came flying over me.

KEY TO SUCCESS
LIMIT DISTRACTIONS

We had minimal distractions. We lived in a small, rather isolated town, with no fast-food restaurants, movie theaters, or other forms of entertainment. The runners didn't have demanding jobs, cell phones, social media, or video games to distract them.

They were teenagers, and teenagers are silly sometimes, even if they were otherwise disciplined. If they wanted to blow off some steam, I wasn't going to make a big deal out of it. And they always cleaned the bus after we returned from trips.

Across our trips and races against new opponents, Caldwell's runners were learning how to stick together. At a dual meet with Newcomerstown, Tony, P.J., and Danny tied for first place and were officially credited with finishing simultaneously. The next three runners were all from Caldwell: Stacy, Brian, and Randy. Chris Fleming crossed the finish line at seventh place, with the first Newcomerstown runner almost two minutes behind Tony. The result was another perfect 15, to a score of 50 for the Trojans.

We were flying high. No teams caught us, but insects were another story. About 20 minutes before our next race, at the Brookville Invitational, P.J. was stung by a bee. He looked like he'd gone 10 rounds of boxing. I didn't want him to race, but P.J. insisted.

IN P.J.'S OWN WORDS I felt a bee in my mouth, and I put my finger in there to get it out, and it stung me under my lip. It swelled up about the size of a golf ball. I was uncomfortable, and it made it difficult to breathe.

I wasn't expecting much. But I picked up as we went along and actually had a pretty good race.

That meet was notable for another reason — for the first and only time, a race director did not allow us to move up to the AAA race. We found out when we arrived at the meet that we would have to race against Class A schools instead. The team was angry and used their frustrations to fuel their performance.

It turned out to be a record-setting day. Not only did the boys score their fourth perfect 15 of their last five events, but in doing so, two of the Caldwell runners broke the existing course record.

P.J., despite the bee sting, bettered the old mark at 15:31 and Tony set the new course record of 15:22. Closing out the top five were Brian, Danny, and Stacy.

The *Daily Jeffersonian* announced the Ohio Association of Cross Country Coaches' rankings in its September 27 issue, placing us at the top of the list of Class A teams. The boys received all 10 first-place votes, giving us the maximum score of 100. We were the only team in any classification to sweep all of the first-place votes, and we held the top place in the standings for the remainder of the season.

But we'd been in these sorts of positions before. The accolades were nice, but we just had to go out and perform.

And our next big test was looming with the Malone College Invitational, one of the state's largest and most prestigious competitions. It featured 30–40 college teams and was a great opportunity for the high school runners to watch what their competition would look like at the collegiate level.

Malone was a huge meet, on par with Tiffin from earlier on the race calendar. The best teams always raced at Malone, making this the second major test of the season. Tiffin and Malone, in addition to the postseason, represented pillars and measuring sticks.

Despite our success, other teams didn't quite believe in our talent. Maybe we didn't quite believe in it yet, either.

We were confident, but this was *Malone.* The next level. The best of the best. And given our success throughout the season, we entered with a bullseye square on our backs. At Tiffin, our runners didn't quite know what to expect. Innocence was bliss. For Malone, the nervous energy had turned to pressure to show up and run well.

We entered the meet's Division IV, where we ran against 28 teams, all of which were from the big-school Class AAA division. That meant these were the most competitive of the large schools. Four of those teams (top-ranked Mentor, no. 3 Toledo St. Francis, no. 4 Youngstown Boardman, and no. 5 Cincinnati Anderson) were ranked among Class AAA's top five at the time.

As with our defining win at Tiffin earlier in the year, this field was deeper and stronger than anything we'd face in the state meet. Tiffin was a revelation. But maybe it was a blip. Maybe someone was missing their best runners that day. I don't think the rest of the state believed that we were the real deal. They didn't respect us yet.

Malone was a chance for us to prove how good we were—to silence the doubters and naysayers for good. And it was a chance for us to reinforce that maybe we weren't too small to win, after all.

IN TONY'S OWN WORDS After moving up classes, we began to realize just how massive the schools were. Our group of eight guys was just a small part of a school with 340 students. In contrast, Mentor, one of the largest high schools in Ohio, had about 2,800 students, which is more than 50% larger than our entire town!

Malone's course had some challenging hills, but nothing as difficult as the ones we faced in practice.

Yet again, Tony finished first, 18 seconds ahead of the next finisher.

P.J. finished fifth, followed by Danny in 14th, Stacy in 24th, and Brian in 34th. While the team's total of 78 points was the highest of the entire season, it was still enough to win the race ahead of second-place (and defending Class AAA state runner-up) Cincinnati Elder and its 129 points, as well as Mentor, which finished third with 136 points.

IN BRIAN'S OWN WORDS Warming up there was a completely different vibe than at Tiffin. Teams weren't making snide remarks and they weren't laughing and joking. We could tell we had poked the bear. The

> nonbelievers were out to show that Tiffin was a fluke.
> Malone's win was a real turning point for our team
> but also changed how other teams in Ohio viewed us.
> The pendulum had swung!

We defeated all 27 of the AAA teams in the event, including almost the whole AAA state-ranked top 10—the most notable being no. 1 Mentor. And we won by a convincing 51 points.

It was early in the season and we'd already beaten a strong AAA field - twice. There were no more doubts from others about Caldwell, no more taunts that we were too small or didn't belong. We had proven ourselves worthy. This wasn't a fluke. All of those Goliaths that had initially looked down on us were now in our rearview mirror. And as it turned out, they weren't all that close.

In just six weeks, we went from a team that was looked down on, a team that opponents didn't think belonged, to a team that other teams

Sophomore Brian Norris

feared. We'd gone from a team that was still finding its way to a team with confidence.

There was no question anymore about how good we were. We'd served notice to the state by beating the top AAA teams. But we still had something to prove. We still had a championship to win. And we hadn't won it yet.

We were reminded of the target on our backs—and the new gear we'd reached—at the Coaches' Classic, held at Cleveland's Edgewater Park along the shores of Lake Erie.

For the previous two years, it had pretty consistently been Tony and P.J. leading the pack. But starting with the Coaches' Classic, Brian emerged as our third runner—which brought a new element to our race strategy. Teams can still beat you if you have two top finishers, depending on how the rest of your team winds up. But adding a third runner to that mix made us that much tougher to beat.

> IN TONY'S OWN WORDS During our interval workouts, things got really competitive between P.J., Brian, and me. P.J. and Brian were both really strong, with Brian being a fierce kicker and sprinter. The three of us would often push each other to the limit. Having them right there alongside me really motivated me to give it my all.

Those three runners meant the difference at the Coaches' Classic, which was held on a cold day and included a race across the sand.

Tony finished first, while Mentor's Eric Ashton and Jerry Fresenko finished second and third. But with P.J. finishing fifth and Brian ninth, we were able to squeak past the top-ranked AAA team, 57–69.

It was our smallest margin of victory that entire year—and it came against a school 8 times our size. It was the type of race we would have struggled to win in 1983 or 1984.

With each successive win, it was getting harder for us to stay under the radar. As the postseason neared, *News-Herald* sportswriter Jim Michels wrote about the Caldwell boys in his "Running Around" column:

"The biggest story in high school cross country this season has been the dominance of tiny Caldwell High School against the toughest big school

Bonfire for the Team **L To R** Stacy Huffman, Tony Carna, Brian Norris, J.D. Secrest, Randy Lowe, Arnie Ferguson, Danny Lowe

competition Ohio can offer... . The widely-traveled Class A Redskins have now easily won eight invitationals this year, including the big school division at the Malone Invitational two weeks ago and the top category at the NEO Coaches Classic at Edgewater Park last Saturday... . Barring a bus breakdown on the way to Columbus, in three weeks the Redskins should easily win the first of two consecutive state championships." [11]

I wanted to pump the brakes on that suggestion. It was all too soon to talk about championships, especially after the "road to state" became a little bit longer. In previous years, teams only needed to run in the district competition to qualify for the state meet in Columbus, but in 1985, a regional meet was added after the district run.

My plan to run against the much bigger Class AAA schools went better than expected. I wanted us to move up so we could better challenge ourselves—*but we still didn't lose!* Now, the postseason loomed. Our chance to erase the heartbreak of seasons past was here, again.

11 Jim Michels, "Tiny Caldwell heads class of Ohio Cross Country," *The News-Herald* (Willoughby, OH), Oct. 7, 1985.

After facing down so many bigger schools and dominating our competition so thoroughly, we had to remain focused on the task at hand. We had to maintain our composure, even as we prepared to face Class A schools again.

First, district.

Second, regional.

Third, state.

IN TONY'S OWN WORDS We were cautious going into the district meet. After experiencing the success in the '85 season, we still knew from the prior seasons that nothing was guaranteed, and if we had a bad day, there would be no chance for the elusive state title. I focused on safely navigating the start, establishing my position, and securing the win.

Maybe it was the sting of the last two state meet losses, but this team was laser-focused. They were ready for this moment.

The team was also well rested. In the three weeks before the start of the postseason, we started to dial back the mileage and work more on speed as part of our "peaking phase." We also stopped weight training. I focused on three-week increments because that's the timeline of when the human body adapts to new stresses.

By reducing mileage and increasing speed workouts, our bodies were readied to run faster during the most important three weeks of the cross country calendar—district, regional, and state.

IN P.J.'S OWN WORDS We were ready because of three main reasons: coaching, experience, and hunger. We were extremely well coached, and we knew it. We'd been there and done that. We knew what losing felt like and we hated it. The postseason was our time to shine.

This approach and preparation paid off nicely in the district race. The boys blew away the competition in a nearly flawless race.

Tony finished in his by-now-usual first-place spot, followed by the Norris brothers: P.J. just nine seconds behind in second place, and Brian in third place. Scott Childers of Zanesville Rosecrans broke up the clean sweep by finishing fourth, but right behind him were Stacy and Danny in fifth and sixth.

So much for worrying about a mental lapse…

Caldwell's score of 17 captured us the district championship ahead of second-place Zanesville Rosecrans at 53. By virtue of that 1–2 finish, our two teams advanced to the regional race the following week at Lancaster High School.

As we advanced to regionals, we weren't in the best of health. Our seventh runner, Chris Fleming, was out altogether after twisting his ankle in practice, while Danny had been nursing a bad back for much of the season.

> IN DANNY'S OWN WORDS We were all running through some sort of pain. You had to suck it up. I sucked it up for the team. I always have and I always would. And I was happy that I ran half-decent at the end of the year, even while being hurt.

We stressed the need for runners to feel discomfort and push through it— it's how they improved and reached new levels. We embraced discomfort, and because of our fitness level, we tried to force other runners out of their comfort zones when they tried to keep pace with us.

Danny's back pain was one of the few times one of our runners faced real, actual pain. We cut down on injuries with proper training, including the right mix of mileage, weight training, and preventative drills.

Our base miles—the 500 Mile Club—meant that when we hit the stressful part of the season, the runners' bodies were prepared and responded accordingly. We also focused on our pre- and post-workout and race routines.

Those tactics came in handy for the regional meet, where we faced off against seven other teams, with the top three advancing to state.

We had our first five runners finish among the top eight in the team race. Posting a score of 25, we finished far ahead of second-place Zanesville

Rosecrans and third-place Newark Catholic. All three teams qualified for the state meet.

Tony won the regional competition, P.J. placed fourth, Brian finished next, in fifth place, Stacy came in seventh, and Danny rounded out Caldwell's top five in eighth place.

Only one race remained—the one we'd been thinking about all year long.

After losing in the 1983 Class A state championship race by just two points, and by only one point in the 1984 title race, losing in 1985 was not an option. We'd run against the top 10 AAA teams and beat them. We knew we had the ability.

> IN TONY'S OWN WORDS It felt like we'd lost the state championship on a half-court buzzer-beating shot two years in a row. And when we returned in 1985, it was a "take no prisoners" attitude. We didn't want it to be close.

Despite a steady drizzle and a temperature in the upper-50s, a crowd estimated to be about 10,000 strong was on hand on November 2, 1985, to watch six state championship races at a new location for the state meet: Scioto Downs Raceway, a horse racetrack a few miles south of Columbus. In fact, I helped design the course as a part of a volunteer group of coaches from the Ohio Association of Track and Cross Country Coaches.

The Class A race came down to experience. The way the course was laid out, its first half mile had the runners going past the grandstands. Early on, as the spectators cheered, Newbury High School's runners held down the first four positions.

But we had our race to run, and another team's approach wasn't going to cause us to change our strategy. As I often told the runners, "Control the race that you run, and only the race you run."

With three-quarters of the race yet to go, the too-fast start proved to be fatal to the Black Knights. The Newbury runners started to fall back, while our core gradually moved to the front.

The course was wet and muddy, and the race finished on the track.

As with all of our meets, I designed a plan that positioned me at three different spots along the course to cheer on the runners and give them

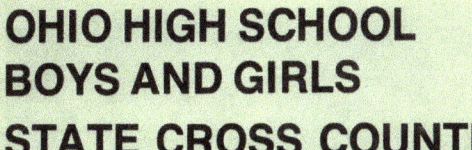

OHIO HIGH SCHOOL
BOYS AND GIRLS
STATE CROSS COUNTRY MEETS

Scioto Downs
November 2, 1985

OFFICIAL PROGRAM $1.50

Richard L. Armstrong, Commissioner

Fred Dafler, Associate Commissioner

Blair C. Irvin, Assistant Commissioner

Clair Muscaro, Assistant Commissioner

Dolores A. Billhardt, Assistant Commissioner

Richard D. Termeer, Assistant Commissioner

SPONSORED & CONDUCTED BY
THE OHIO HIGH SCHOOL ATHLETIC ASSOCIATION

Cover — Pam Lewis

1985 State Meet Program

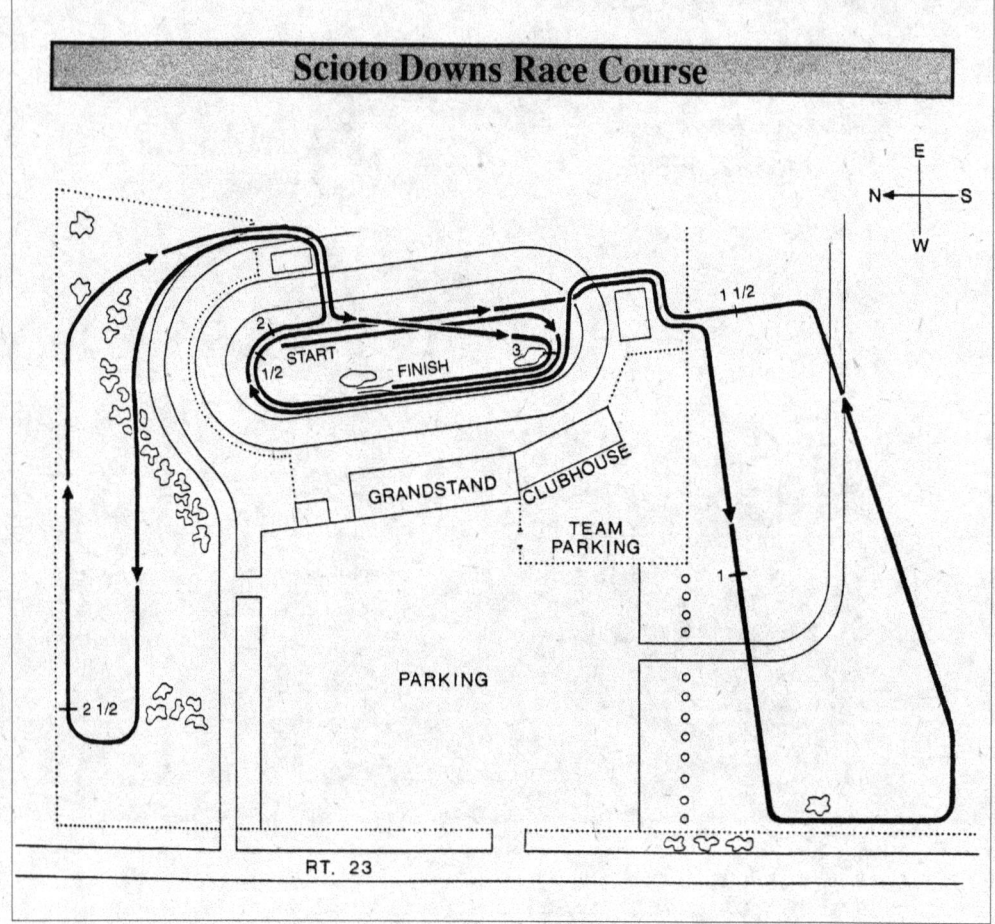

1985 State Meet Course

encouragement to finish the race strong. It also allowed me to see how we were performing as a team and individually. If someone wasn't running great, I could give them a little more support.

I was with the guys at the starting line and the course's south loop before sprinting across the parking lot to see them in the north loop, then positioned myself toward the finish line, where I could see the runners coming in from the north field for the last 600 meters of the race.

From that spot, I saw Tony run past in the first spot...

And P.J. third...

And Brian sixth...

And Danny seventh...

We needed a strong finish from our fifth runner—it was a heartbreaking lesson we'd learned at the previous state championship meet, when Danny got dehydrated and faded out of contention near the finish line.

We needed Stacy to finish strong. But after his leg cramped up around the half-mile mark of the race, he was struggling.

It felt all too familiar.

But Stacy kept gritting it out and kept running, courageously fighting his way to finish in 16th place.

As Stacy sprinted past me, I could smile and breathe a sigh of relief. There wasn't any doubt. No counting needed. No heartbreaking loss. No last-second surprise.

1+3+6+7+16=33.

The fast-starting Black Knights of Newberry finished with a score of 93, a whopping 60 points behind the Class A state champions from Caldwell High School.

We did it! We finally did it!

The Caldwell boys huddled near the finish line on the inside of the horse track. They stood in an ankle-deep puddle and locked arms, congratulating each other and basking in the moment. They'd overcome so much: the disappointment of coming so close twice, bouts of heatstroke and bee stings, bumps and bruises and back pain, and endless challenges from bigger teams that looked down on us and didn't quite believe we were all that good. But we did it! And here we were, standing tall.

Caldwell's runners had waited two long years for this. And they achieved their goal in convincing fashion.

> IN P.J.'S OWN WORDS The monkey was off our back, and that was huge. We smiled in elation. We were muddy, and we didn't even care. That was one of the best moments.

This was truly something special. Our boys had run an incredible, record-setting race, with four runners among the top 10 finishers, the first time any team had accomplished that feat. (Three of those runners, Tony, P.J., and Brian, earned All-Ohio honors.)

Four of our runners finished before any other team's second runner crossed the finish line.

In winning the race, Tony became the first Class A runner in the state to ever win back-to-back state championship races.

1985 Ohio State Meet Champions on podium

1985 Team: Front L To R Assistant Coach Dugan Hill, J.D. Secrest, Chris Fleming, John Garrett, Head Coach Ron Martin **Back L To R** Danny Lowe, Brian Norris, Randy Lowe, P.J. Norris, Tony Carna, Stacy Huffman, Brian Robinson

IN BRIAN'S OWN WORDS In the regular season, we proved we were the best team in the state, but we still had not won a state championship. It was the mission of the team, and it was amazing to see our intense focus. We were there for one job and acted that way. When I look back over the years, I am still amazed we didn't take things for granted and goof off more. We cruised through wins with unbelievable drive and determination to prove we were the best.

One of the Caldwell team's preseason goals had been to be the best cross country team in the state, and on this day—and in every race we'd run that season—we were. Our winning 33 points was the lowest score of any of the six victorious teams that day, regardless of class. Our score tied the 1970 team from Kent State University School for the lowest-ever Class A state meet point total.

In fact, our times were faster than any other team's times, in any division. That means that we effectively beat every team at the state meet that year, including teams from some of the largest schools in Ohio.

> IN TONY'S OWN WORDS During the podium ceremony, it felt like we had won the Super Bowl. The stands were packed with Caldwell supporters, and they were really loud. It was an amazing experience, and it was hard to leave the podium because of how great it felt.

When we returned home later that day, a crowd of well-wishers welcomed us home. The crowd cheered the boys as the runners looped around the square in a fire truck. The runners felt like rock stars. This was their moment. They'd accomplished the goal that had eluded us, the state championship that had been just out of reach. But this wasn't just about winning one time, it was about building a dynasty.

We weren't finished. No, the race for greatness had only begun.

PART V
RACE FOR GREATNESS: 1986

12.

WHEN EXCELLENCE IS IN SIGHT, GOOD IS NOT ENOUGH

It's hard to repeat as champions.

Sports history is littered with great teams that should have repeated but didn't. Teams lose focus or get cocky or get complacent or pull back on their training.

Sometimes athletes lose sight of a team-first mentality and focus more on themselves. Sometimes the dynamics don't work the second time around, or injuries pile up.

Some teams just get lazy.

But not this team. Letting up wasn't an option.

As I constantly told the runners, "When excellence is in sight, good is not enough." They embodied that saying during the summer leading up to the 1986 season.

The team had overcome every challenge the season before, beating all of the Class AAA schools we ran against and picking up the state championship in dominating fashion.

Now was a chance for a repeat—the race for greatness.

There wasn't a moment when a runner took their foot off the gas, loafed, or cut corners. There was still so much for this team to accomplish.

Despite winning the state championship in 1985, we hadn't even accomplished three of our five team goals: have five runners in the top 15 in all invitationals and all seven runners in the top 30; win the state championship with less than 30 points (we were close, with 33); and earn All-Ohio honors for five runners (we had three).

We were good in 1985—really good. But we wanted to be great. And we hadn't reached our full potential yet.

KEY TO SUCCESS
NEVER SETTLE

It was not enough to just be good. I gave
my athletes the confidence to believe in themselves
and never stopped pushing them. I wanted to make
sure they never settled for anything less
than excellence.

The work ethic from the previous summer was still there, but this time around the runners seemed to be having more fun and running more freely. The weight was off their shoulders.

It helped having a core of upperclassmen—we'd gone from one of the youngest teams in Ohio in 1983 and 1984 to one of the oldest and most experienced. Tony, P.J., and Randy were entering their senior year and represented speed, leadership, and heart. Juniors Brian, Danny, and Stacy were right there with them—proven, experienced runners with lots of miles and success behind them.

That year would be the group's last chance to race together as teammates, and I vowed to send them off in a legendary manner.

Joining our veteran team was freshman Steve "Arnie" Ferguson, the latest in a long line of Fergusons to run for Caldwell. He was one of the best junior high runners in the state in 1985, certainly in Class A. He moved up to the varsity team in 1986 and looked to become a key component of the team.

Just like his older brothers Randy (known as "Poke") and Deuce, Steve had a nickname of his own, "Arnie." His enormous appetite as a baby reminded his older sister Jo Ellen of Arnold the Pig from the show *Green Acres*, which was popular at the time. Hence, Arnie.

By the time Arnie was a freshman, we better understood the value of controlling and limiting the younger runners' miles. I wanted to conserve his potential. We only allowed him to run 350 miles when we were running the 500 Mile Club, bumping him up to 500 miles in subsequent seasons. He even made the 600 Mile Club his senior year. He was also a four-year starter in basketball, so he wasn't able to participate in our winter clubs, only the summer ones.

IN ARNIE'S OWN WORDS By the time I came in as a freshman, I was itching to run that 500 Mile Club, but Coach Ron didn't allow me to do so. He felt that my two older brothers overtrained, so he wanted to hold me back a little and restricted me that first year. By the time I got there, a lot of things were done differently.

More than anything, I cherished getting the opportunity to hang out with the juniors and seniors as a freshman. I really looked up to them, and it was a big deal for a kid just trying to find his place on the team. The fact that I could be a part of a group that was bigger than myself—a group that was well defined and respected—meant the world to me.

I remember the start to Arnie's running career years earlier like it was yesterday. He was in elementary school when we went up to the Tiffin Columbian Cross Country Carnival, which had an elementary race that preceded the main event. About 15 minutes before the race, I said, "Hey Arnie, do you want to run this?"

It was 1,000 meters long. He jumped right in and tore it apart, defeating the entire field.

From that point on, he was hooked, and he went on to do amazing things for Caldwell, in college, and in his career beyond.

Adding Arnie to the team ensured there would be continuity for the program in the years ahead as some of our marquee runners graduated. It was as though we'd brought on the Tony of the future. And the Tony of the present could teach a lot to the team's future leader—namely, how to work hard, do things the right way, and win.

Caldwell's record over the past three years was an incredible 398–2, with our only two losses, by a total of three points, in the Class A state finals. (Those losses *still* hurt, even to this day.)

With a team so experienced and so talented, I could train them at the highest level and focus on more advanced strategies that developed their mental toughness.

We focused on how to attack hills and then surge – picking up the pace—at the top, when everyone else was trying to catch their breath, to play on opponents' minds and rattle them. I taught them to surge around turns, too. When you run with a pack, you get comfortable. But you need to get uncomfortable at times to break away from the pack. To do that, you need to take your opponents out of their comfort zone. Building our runners' mental toughness would give us an edge, and it addressed one of our team's few weak spots from the previous season.

On race day, I coached them to go out strong—but not too strong—and pick off runners who went out too hard or spent too much energy early. We trained, too, on how to deal with side stitches and muscle cramps and continue pushing through the pain.

By getting comfortable with being uncomfortable, by pushing a little bit harder, we inched closer and closer to greatness.

The 1986 season was a chance to etch our names into the record books. We could be a one hit wonder, but we wanted to build something lasting - a culture and a legacy.

So the boys got to work on authoring a new chapter.

That new chapter formally began that summer with the TAC Junior Olympics in Nebraska, where four of our top seven runners competed in distance events.

1986 Postcard Lincoln, Nebraska

With a time of 15:41.67, Brian finished second in the 5,000-meter run in the 15–16-year-old age group. It bested his personal record by nearly 24 seconds and earned him All-America honors. He also ran in the 1,500-meter race, and after finishing eighth in a preliminary heat, he finished 10th in the finals.

Danny was a double All-America winner in Nebraska. In the 2,000-meter steeplechase, he finished third. He then ran in the 10,000-meter race in the 15–16-year-old group and finished second, while Stacy and PJ earned

All-America honors by finishing fifth and seventh in the 17–18-year-old age group, respectively.

Dail Harper, Caldwell's standout shot-putter, was once again an all-American and earned his second national runner-up in the 17–18-year-old group.

As we headed into the season, as usual, I set some lofty preseason goals for the coming season:

- Have five runners in the top 15 in all invitationals and all seven runners in the top 30
- Win the Pioneer Valley Conference Championship
- Win the district and regional competitions with fewer than 25 points
- Win the state championships with fewer than 33 points
- Five runners to receive All-Ohio honors

My goals were purposefully meant to be tough, and borderline unrealistic, to keep us out of our comfort zone. With a year under our belts of running up a division, I also had a better idea of how to set goals for this season.

This team had to keep digging and stay focused in order to avoid getting complacent—which was getting increasingly harder as the wider cross country world was starting to recognize our success.

Ahead of the season, the *Harrier* magazine, the leading national cross country publication, ranked us the number two team in the country behind the Woodlands High School in Texas. It was huge news for any team, especially one from a tiny town in rural southeast Ohio. These types of things just didn't happen in our corner of the world. For a comparison, the Woodlands had more kids in their high school than people in our entire town!

I tried to downplay the ranking. I didn't want the runners to believe the hype or to feel like they had arrived and lose sight of their goals.

Excellence was in sight, and good was not enough—especially not for this team.

13.

CHASING A LEGACY

Following our summer training, the boys' season kicked off at the end of August with the Newcomerstown Invitational: six Class AAA teams … and Caldwell.

We were not going to sneak up on anyone this time around. Everyone else—across the state and now the country—knew how talented we were. After we moved up to face tougher competition the year earlier, and beat all comers, these teams had a year to prepare to race us again. The success and attention and state championship meant everyone was gunning for us, especially the big schools. They were tired of being upstaged by little Caldwell.

We had a target on our backs—and the hunter became the hunted.

It also remained to be seen how the squad would respond to the weight of success. It's one thing to be hungry to win. It's another thing entirely to stay hungry after you've reached the pinnacle—to keep working and improving, even with all the hype and attention.

That wasn't a problem at Newcomerstown. We placed four runners among the first six, and all seven in the top 12, to score a 24–45 win over second-place New Philadelphia.

Next up was the Akron Firestone Invitational. Sticking to our past strategy, we were the only Class A team in a field of AAA opponents.

L To R Junior Stacy Huffman, Seniors: Randy Lowe, Tony Carna and P.J. Norris

The race started with a quarter mile of open field, followed by a 90-degree turn and a dash up a hill. Our starting box was in the middle, so we had runners on both sides of us. (Sometimes we would be closer to the ends.) This, coupled with the turn, made for a challenging start. Runners needed to get out well and get to the turn in a good position to attack the hill.

Our runners getting elbowed and having runners pinch down on their lane at the start of the race didn't help. When Caldwell moved up to face bigger schools, lots of teams were respectful. But not all of them. It wasn't uncommon for a team's sixth and seventh runners to throw elbows at the start of the race—they didn't have anything to lose—and for bigger runners to pinch down on both sides of us.

That wasn't our style. We were more interested in letting our legs do the talking. But in times of conflict and sharp elbows, Tony often turned to Brian as an enforcer and protector. Brian didn't mind throwing elbows when the situation called for it.

> **IN TONY'S OWN WORDS** This is one of the races that was a huge elbow match for several hundred yards. Sometimes the teams on one or both sides would pinch down on our lane. The closer our starting assignment was to the middle of the field, the wilder it got.

Tony endured the elbows and the turn and the hill to cross the finish line first, just seconds ahead of a pair of runners from New Philadelphia High School, Frank Fry and Brad Whitis. It was one of the few races where two runners from another school broke our top two.

P.J. and Stacy were fourth and fifth, respectively, with Brian, Randy, and Danny finishing within five seconds of each other in eighth through 10th. When the points were totaled, Caldwell finished first ahead of New Philadelphia by a convincing 27–63 margin.

The 1986 season was starting exactly how we'd planned, with us running well against some of the state's top teams.

But another major challenge loomed: Tiffin. A total of 110 teams and nearly 2,500 runners were on hand for what would be one of the biggest races of the entire regular season. As the Tiffin newspaper noted, "About 500 more runners participated in the Carnival than there are residents of Caldwell."[12]

It was a completely loaded field: twenty-one AAA schools and us. Our focus was Cincinnati Elder, the fifth-ranked team in the nation, which had already beaten Trinity, a nationally ranked school out of Kentucky.

A year ago at this very race, we were viewed as an afterthought and "too small to win." But as we warmed up at Tiffin this time, there was a different feeling—one of admiration. There were no more comments about us being too small. We were the alpha, the team to beat. Other teams scoped us out as we jogged the course and stretched, pointing at us and saying, "That's them; that's Caldwell." Our reputation preceded us.

---

[12] Barry Peters, "The Caldwell Connection," *The Advertiser-Tribune* (Tiffin, OH), September 14, 1986.

This gave us confidence—instead of the butterflies of a year before—as the runners positioned themselves at the starting line. The butterflies had been transferred to runners from other, bigger schools.

It helped having optimum race conditions—a much more pleasant experience than the sweltering heat we'd endured in 1985.

POW! The gun sounded and the race began. Caldwell established a good pace. The runners attacked hills and surged, just as we'd practiced, moving up spots in big chunks as the race entered the second mile.

The runners were using all the techniques we'd practiced.

As in previous years, I watched from strategic spots, then raced to my final position toward the finish line, putting me in the perfect spot to see the runners emerge over the hill from the lower position.

Last year, we'd finished with three of our runners in the first eight spots. How would we fare this time with so much focus on us? Would another school emerge as the team to beat? Someone was bound to step up and surprise us...

I couldn't believe my eyes as the first runners climbed the hill.

Tony was leading the way in Caldwell red and white, the only runner to break 16 minutes.

Brian and P.J. were right behind him to finish 1-2-3 in a completely loaded field.

Stacy came in seventh, and Randy closed out the Caldwell scorers in 16th. Our score of 29 easily bested second place Cincinnati Elder (81), that year's Class AAA state champions. We had four runners cross the finish line before Elder—coming off a win against nationally ranked Kentucky Trinity—had a single runner finish. In a dual meet against the entire field—against the top five finishers from all the other schools combined—Caldwell would have still won, 29–32.

It's unheard of to beat the field at a massive race like Tiffin, especially since all of the other teams—from far bigger schools—had a year to prepare to face us.

Randy considers it our best race, and he's probably right.

We got all seven runners on the first page of the results. Normally, you're flipping through to the fifth or sixth page to come up with your seventh runner. But our seventh runner was 46th out of about 150 runners!

It made me so proud to see our success, especially since it came at my hometown, with my friends and family and coaching colleagues present. I like to stay humble and try not to get too emotional about any single race, but our performance at Tiffin that year was a goosebumps kind of moment. For the second year in a row, we rode up to Tiffin and put on a show.

Notably, it was the first time Brian beat his brother and the first time in more than a year that someone other than Tony or P.J. finished second in a race. Reaching that level helped Brian break through a mental ceiling and solidified our three-runner attack. The duo at the top of the pack was now a troika—making it that much harder for another team to break through.

Ron Combs, a future cross country/track and field coach for Wilmington College, was waiting in the wings at Tiffin as a non-varsity team member of Tiffin Columbian High School.

"I noticed multiple athletes from the same team near the front of the race. They had these older, worn-out uniforms on, which was in sharp contrast to every other team that had fresh new singlets on," he said. "Even in those worn-out uniforms, I had never before witnessed such a dominant run by a team."

Winning so convincingly attracted more attention. As Barry Peters, the sports editor of *The Advertiser-Tribune* wrote, "Ohio high school cross country revolves around Caldwell."[13]

There was no letdown with this team—and by this point, they were a focused, cohesive unit. The Thursday after the Tiffin Cross Country Carnival, we ran in a quad meet. Accomplishing something that Caldwell had never done before, not only did we sweep the first eight finishing places, but the first seven Caldwell runners— Tony, P.J., Randy, Brian, Stacy, Danny, and Arnie—all finished with the exact same time. Chris was not far behind, placing eighth. With this race, we registered our second perfect score of the season, easily defeating second-place Belpre and its 59 points.

Our schedule sped forward, and as we reached late September, I dialed up the runners' interval workouts, with the goal of building lung capacity

---

13 Ibid.

ahead of our race at Malone, one of the biggest races on our calendar. The weather was starting to turn, and the red and orange leaves brought new color—and new energy—to our workouts. I focused on mile repeats and 880s (half-mile runs), with three or four of each. The real test came from reducing the rest between each interval, a tactic that tested the runners' mental toughness and their ability to run at an elevated heart rate for an extended period of time.

I wanted to challenge and push the guys without destroying their legs for Malone. Our training was a constant balance—being prepared for meets while keeping us fresh for the end of the year.

KEY TO SUCCESS
A GREAT TRAINING PROGRAM

Coaching required finding a sustainable balance. I wasn't afraid to try new things. I continued to learn and experiment, sorting through different strategies until I had developed a training program that worked for my runners. Then I stuck with what worked because I believe "if it ain't broke, don't fix it!"

Despite two good weeks of training, there was a nervous energy ahead of Malone when we found out that Bob Kennedy of Westerville North was running. I'd heard Kennedy had already committed to Indiana University, one of the best midwestern college programs. He was on his way to becoming a national champion, two-time Olympian, and American record holder in the 5,000 meters.

This guy was *fast*. Faster than fast.

Tony was faster than fast, too, but I didn't want to tell him. Tony hadn't lost in 28 races. He was the ultimate competitor, and he was going to do everything he could to keep that streak alive. I didn't want Tony to be psyched out. But I also didn't want him to be surprised.

Learning that Kennedy was racing felt like being late for a very important meeting, and as you pull into the parking lot, there's only one space available and another car pulling into the lot at the same time. Tony and Bob were made from the same mold.

If I had known Tony would be running against Bob Kennedy, I would have rested him and kept him out of a race earlier that week. But that wasn't how it played out.

My assistant coach and I whispered about Kennedy, gushing about his talent. *He's a tough competitor. He's improved so much, and he's doing it on low miles. And his uncle was an All-American for Indiana, and he's probably going to go there, too. He's got good genes. They have a thoroughbred.*

Tony saw us whispering and came over.

"What are you guys talking about?" he asked.

"There's a really good runner in this race," I told him, "but he puts his pants on the same way you do." I talked about Kennedy's lineage and talent. I tried to keep things as simple as possible. I just wanted Tony to run his best race.

After Tony found out that Bob Kennedy was in the race, and Kennedy found out that Tony had moved up to run against him, it was like adding fuel to the fire. They had mutual respect for each other—this was that other runner they'd heard about.

They hated to lose. To both of them, losing was not an option.

The race started downhill for the beginning—a typical Malone race. Tony and Kennedy were separating from the pack. About a mile in, there was a really steep hill.

Kennedy hit that hill hard.

IN TONY'S OWN WORDS He got a gap there, probably three or four seconds. He was incredibly strong up Sign Hill. After that, it was a game of trying to keep it close and I hoped I could make it later.

I was full tilt trying to make up ground, but it was *Bob Kennedy*. He made his move at the mile mark, and I was giving chase, but he was a tough customer and kept pulling away.

Bob Kennedy was a year younger than me, and he finished second in the AAA state race as a sophomore—

his teammate Eric Nelson, who went to Ohio State, beat him. He was great. But the way I saw it, he was beatable.

At that point, there was no reason why I didn't think I could beat him.

The chase was on for the last two miles—two guys digging deep and giving everything they had. Both guys had determined looks on their faces. Every time Tony got close, Kennedy would find a new gear. You would have thought after Bob gapped Tony on Sign Hill that Tony would have thrown in the towel or faded back, but the gap never grew. Like Bob, Tony was out to make a statement.

They came up to the last half mile, and Kennedy was still leading. There was no slowdown, no quit. We were shouting as loud as we could: "SURGE, TONY!" Tony dug as deep as he could.

As Kennedy pulled away from Tony—he'd win by 13 seconds—we had another problem. P.J., our number two runner, started dry-heaving midway through the race and had to stop running. He fell ill, and it didn't look like he would finish the race.

That meant we were in a fight. We were down our number two runner in a race against the strongest field we'd faced. Our win streak was in jeopardy.

I yelled at the other Caldwell runners, "P.J. is out of the race!" They needed to pick up every spot they could. *Every spot mattered*. That was the awful lesson we'd learned in the 1983 and 1984 state championships, when we'd fallen just short.

Danny Lowe—who'd struggled with overheating and other medical issues throughout his cross country career—kicked into gear.

IN DANNY'S OWN WORDS I remember Ron screaming at the top of his lungs, and that sparked me in the last half of the race to try to finish as strongly as I could. I was in pain the whole way. Most of the season I was in pain because of my back and a major growth spurt that caused stress fractures in my hips.

Losing P.J. forced our other runners to dig deeper and endure a little more pain. The team didn't want to let each other down—and we sure as heck didn't want to lose.

Our runners finished strong. Brian was the second Caldwell runner to cross the finish line, in seventh place, with Stacy just eight seconds behind him in 10th place. That gave us three runners among the first 10 finishers, making us the only team with more than one finisher in the top ten. Randy was Caldwell's fourth runner, finishing in 19th place, and his brother Danny closed out the team's top five scorers with a 29th-place finish.

Had P.J. run his typical race, we would have finished with a point total in the mid-40s. Still, we finished the day with 67 points—by far our highest total for the year, but that was little consolation to the other 30 teams in the Division IV race. Our closest competitor, Cincinnati Anderson, was a somewhat distant second with 104 points.

Even with Bob Kennedy being *Bob Kennedy,* even with our second-best runner dropping out, even against a massive field of top Class AAA teams, we were still able to pull out the win by a comfortable margin. As *The Canton Repository* noted, "Caldwell High School continues to be the mouse that roared in Ohio high school cross country."[14]

It was interesting to think about the races we'd lost in the past and how a lack of depth had cost us. Winning the 1986 Malone race showed us how much we'd matured and the power of teamwork. We were truly running as a team. Together, we could rise above *anything*.

Our success was a total team effort—from our top seven runners to the rest of the roster.

The unsung heroes were the members who worked just as hard but never got the chance to break into varsity: Chris Fleming, Brian Robinson, Mark Rex, and Dale Radcliff. The Caldwell team was loaded with hard-working, talented runners, and these four had to be patient and just keep putting in the work needed.

They were as much a part of the team's success as the top seven. The press chooses to dwell on varsity runners, often forgetting additional team members. It's easy to keep moving forward if you are in the limelight all the

---

14 "Tiny Caldwell Winner at Malone," *The Canton Repository*, September 28, 1986.

Top Tony finished 2nd to Bob Kennedy
Bottom Brian finished 7th

Top Stacy finished 10th
Bottom Randy finished 19th

Top Danny finished 29th
Bottom Arnie finished 66th

time. However, it's much more difficult to trudge onward knowing that you just have to keep working smart and patiently wait for your day to shine.

I admire those non-varsity runners because they worked just as hard but rarely got any of the credit. I actually got more excited when I saw those kids' eyes light up after they accomplished something they never thought possible. There was nothing more gratifying than knowing you reached all your runners and helped them to be the best they could be.

It was notable to see how, in three short years, we went from barely forming a team with six runners to flourishing with about a dozen guys. Our success made people interested in joining the team. Success breeds success—and we found strength in numbers.

> IN RANDY'S OWN WORDS Ron would be out on the course yelling, and you could hear him forever. But our JV runners would be staggered along the course and would let us know how we were doing—where we were, our position, or just well-timed information. "You got this guy from this team just ahead of you, think about trying to pick him off." They were contributing to the team in their own ways.

The younger runners' families brought even more support to the cross country program. Since we competed across the state, many of the parents traveled great distances. They also provided lots of nutrition between Thursday night "carb load" dinners and postrace recovery food.

Life wasn't always easy, but the boys' families made sure that nothing got in the way of running. And running made sure these boys had a greater chance to win at life. The support from the parents had a significant impact on this team.

Our success was rubbing off in other ways, too. That season marked the return of Caldwell's girls cross country program, which had been discontinued after the 1981 season. (Kim Singer was All-Ohio that year, but in the seasons that followed, we didn't have enough runners to field a team).

Six female runners ran cross country that season: Barb Lowe (Randy and Danny's sister), Kelly Walters, Renee and Annette Nau, Shannon Koval, and Beth Radcliff.

The boys would start our runs together with the girls, but they would eventually split off. The girls ran intervals with fewer reps and distance runs that were a little bit shorter.

It was encouraging to see how the boys team's success was starting to have a deeper impact in Caldwell, and I was happy to see a group of girls interested in the sport.

> **IN RANDY'S OWN WORDS** Barb is someone I really look up to. She helped restart Caldwell's girls' team. She wasn't the most gifted runner athletically, but she practiced really hard, and she went on and earned a letter at Ohio State, which was a dream of mine. She ran cross country her freshman year, then she applied the work ethic and determination from running to become part of the Ohio State University marching band. She was part of TBDBITL (The Best Damn Band in The Land) and really was an inspiration for our family.

That 1986 girls team was dedicated and worked hard. They wound up winning districts and had a 47–13 record for the season. Their effort laid the groundwork for a girls team that has kept running for all the years since.

While the girls team was finding its way, the boys team was seeking new challenges. That season, we wanted to enter the McQuaid Invitational, the largest Invitational in the United States, held in Rochester, New York. We wanted to test ourselves against the best of the best.

But OHSAA rules barred teams from traveling to events that were more than 250 miles from the school's location, and the McQuaid race happened to be about 375 miles away.

Proving ourselves outside of Ohio would have been nice. Instead, we set our sights on the state's top programs.

We headed north to the shores of Lake Erie at Edgewater Park for another shot at the Coaches' Classic. We were running in the boys' Division III race against 17 Class AAA opponents, the best that the North Coast had to offer, including the defending Class AAA state champions from Mentor High School.

The weather and course conditions left a lot to be desired. Rain moved in the afternoon of the race, turning the course muddy in places and making the runners' footing tricky. Even in the slop, our boys proceeded as if it were business as usual.

That race—in the pounding rain, with the wind whipping up—was all about mental toughness. The weather conditions were awful, but I never let the runners make an excuse.

Tony led the pack, finishing 26 seconds ahead of any other runner. One commentator called his time "astonishing," considering the condition of the course.[15] P.J. finished third, with his brother Brian just behind him in fourth place. Stacy came in ninth, while Randy closed out the Caldwell scoring in 13th place. The team's total of 30 points easily defeated Mentor and its 96 points—and this after Mentor had just run its best race of the season.

That performance put an exclamation point on our season. We'd faced down the state's top cross country teams at Tiffin, Malone, and now the Coaches' Classic—and dominated.

On that day, we swept both the boys' and the girls' races, with a headline in one newspaper recognizing us: "Caldwell Class of Coaches' Classic."[16]

After the Coaches' Classic, sportswriter Jim Michels of the *The News-Herald* expressed what many were thinking:

"Caldwell
The very word has taken on an almost religious significance
in Ohio cross country circles.
Caldwell
The name is whispered reverently by the legion of Redskin
followers who have become true believers in the last two seasons.
Caldwell
The city is destined to become a shrine for distance coaches and
runners who have witnessed the miracles that Coach Ron Martin
has produced in a school with just 340 students.

---

15 Jim Michels, "Caldwell Class of Coaches' Classic," *The News-Herald* (Willoughby, OH), October 5, 1986.
16 Ibid.

For the second year in a row, the Caldwell Redskins of Southeastern Ohio trounced the best cross country runners this part of the state could offer in the Coaches' Classic ... . The Redskins, who have crisscrossed Ohio in recent years in search of competition, were frustrated at Edgewater. Their main problem is that there simply is no competition for them in Ohio, and possibly not in the entire country.

[After] seeing the [Caldwell] boys run away with the Division III title yesterday, Kenston Coach Frank Gibas could not imagine a better high school team. Gibas should be a fair judge of distance runners, having seen his teams win a state championship and finish among the top four in the last five Class AA state meets.

Need more evidence? Mentor Coach Jim Green conceded that his runners were shooting for second place at the start of the race. 'We knew we were running for second,' Green explained, '[with] Caldwell in the race.'"[17]

Days later, the weekly Ohio Cross Country Coaches state poll was published in *The Daily Jeffersonian*, placing us at the top of the Class A rankings with a perfect 100 points.[18] We were the only team, boys or girls, to garner all of the first-place votes in its class.

The regular season was quickly drawing to a close. We won the Zanesville Invitational in October, narrowly missing a perfect score. Before the race, P.J., ever the caring person, decided to donate blood—which definitely didn't help his time! No wonder he only beat Brian by one second.

In our final meet before the three-week run to state, we completely dominated the other four teams in the Pioneer Valley Conference Championship. With the temperature hovering near 50 under a cloudy sky, Tony again broke the course record on our home turf with a time of 15:37, followed by P.J., Brian, Randy, and Stacy for our fifth perfect score of the season.

---

17 Ibid.
18 "Ohio High School Cross Country Coaches Poll," *The Daily Jeffersonian* (Cambridge, OH), October 10, 1986.

Blueprint for 1986
Cross Country Season

1986 INVITATIONAL AND POSTSEASON MEETS

MEET LOCATION	SCORE	WINS
Newcomerstown Invitational	24 pts.	6-0
Akron Firestone Invitational	27 pts.	10-0
Tiffin Cross Country Carnival	29 pts.	21-0
Brookville Invitational	25 pts.	8-0
Malone College Invitational	67 pts.	30-0
Lakewood Coaches Classic	30 pts.	17-0
Zanesville Invitational	16 pts.	8-0
PVC League Meet - Caldwell	15 pts	4-0
District Meet - Cambridge	16 pts	6-0
Regional Meet - Lancaster	19 pts.	9-0
State Championship Meet - Columbus	26 pts.	11-0
Overall Season Record (including dual meets)		137-0

The 1-2-3-4-5 finish marked our 38th consecutive invitational victory over the last four years.

After four years of dominating our competition, more and more people in Caldwell recognized how special this team was. The football team took two buses to watch us run, and Coach Mike Devol brought the team out in their pads. Alan Murrey and Shane Hall, two high school classmates and dear friends to the team, even had a video camera on an ATV out in front of the runners, recording the team in action.

IN RANDY'S OWN WORDS It was special for me when the football team came out to watch us, and redemption played into that. I was bullied years earlier by the football team and quit, and now I was doing something that made them take notice. But there was also forgiveness. Many of the players on the team were and are dear friends of mine, and it was powerful for me to let go of my emotions. The only way I knew how to fight back from being bullied was through running, and here we were running our way into the record books. It meant a lot for me to move on from that, but also to find a team that would lift me and help me be my best, and I found that in cross country.

When the cross country state rankings came out later that same week, we had retained our perfect 100-point first-place ranking in Class A.

We were undefeated for the regular season—again—and ready for the path to the state competition. It was time to cement our legacy.

As the regular season wound down, we shifted our approach to focus on speed. The final weeks of the regular season brought gut-wrenching speed workouts—they were so intense, the runners felt like they were going to throw up. These runs were all about survival.

That race for greatness was most evident in our cemetery runs, which had so much meaning to our team. The runners would complete quarter-mile loops, and when they came around that final corner, it was like Churchill Downs—a horse race along this narrow track, three runners wide with challengers nipping at their heels, elbows and snot flying, *and down the stretch they come!*

Down the stretch, the last 200 meters or so, when we turned the corner, the guys hammered down with five or six of them going at it, all out, not letting up an inch.

Our workouts in the cemetery brought out the best in our team while connecting us more deeply on some cosmic plane and reminding us of a thing we didn't want to think about: This team's time running together was finite and fleeting. A high school athlete's glory passes in the blink of an eye. Four years go like *that,* and then it's on to other things.

Even after achieving so much, after winning the state title and getting national recognition, this team wanted more. They embraced the hard runs because they knew it challenged them to be their best.

Not only were they talented and experienced, but their mental toughness meant they pushed through *everything.* There was no quit and no letup on the road to a repeat.

Our first step toward another state championship was the Class A Eastern District meet at the Cambridge State Hospital.

It was a chilly October morning in the low 40s when the teams arrived at the course. It was a *slooooooooow* course with the grass cut high. Tony was in front once the race kicked off and P.J. was right behind him, as they almost always were.

A quarter mile to go. The last trip across the road. Just as we planned.

Until a blue Chevy pickup came out of nowhere, almost slamming into both of them. Tony was at the front of the truck. P.J. was near the truck's back end.

> IN TONY'S OWN WORDS The truck almost hit me, and I slammed the hood with my open hand, and the driver panicked and hit the brakes.

> IN P.J.'S OWN WORDS I was two or three seconds behind Tony. After the truck almost hit us, Tony went around the front right of it and I went behind the back left of it.

Thankfully, neither of them was injured. But it was a scary moment.

Even with the Chevy pickup almost ruining everything, we still dominated the rest of the competition. Tony, P.J., and Brian led the way. Randy finished next, followed by Rob Miller from Zanesville Rosecrans High School, and nipping at his heels just one second later was Arnie in sixth place. Stacy (eighth) and Danny (10th) made sure that all seven Caldwell runners finished in the top 10.

We defeated second-place Zanesville Rosecrans, 16–70. The team's 16 points was the lowest point total ever recorded for an Eastern District meet.

Pretty good for us, given the close call.

The next race, the Class A regional meet at Lancaster High School, matched us up against a field of 10 teams. The weather at race time had the temperature in the upper 50s under a cloudy sky. While it did not rain that day, the course was still a bit sloppy.

Thankfully, there were no vehicles to dodge this time!

Tony led from start to finish, as usual. As sportswriter Kenny Clouse noted in *The Daily Jeffersonian*, Tony "was never really challenged. His time had to make spectators wonder what kind of a time he could have turned in if he was pushed and the course was not wet and muddy."[19]

As it was, Tony set a new course record with a time of 15:45, a full 15 seconds off the previous mark. P.J. was second and Brian third to give Caldwell a sweep of the first three spots. Finishing sixth and seventh in the team competition were Randy and Stacy. The Caldwell score of 19 points not only won for the team the regional race, but it also broke the previous record low score by two points.

The victory granted us the honor of competing in the Class A state meet once again. The competition was held in Columbus. We faced off against second-place Worthington Christian (72 points at regional) and third-place Rosecrans (104 points at regional).

Again, we had the bullseye on our backs. And if we needed a reminder of that, when the final Ohio Cross Country Coaches Poll came out, we

---

19 Kenny Clouse, "Regional Titles for Colts, 'Skins," *The Daily Jeffersonian* (Cambridge, OH), October 27, 1986.

were right where we had been all season: first place in Class A, with a perfect score of 100.[20]

The boys state championship was held on November 1, once again at Scioto Downs Raceway. All of our hard work, four years of excellence, culminated in one final race.

I was so incredibly proud of this team. They believed in each other and worked to better themselves and their teammates every day. Here we were on the threshold of greatness. We needed the state championship to put a punctuation mark on our dominance.

During warm-ups, about 20 minutes before the start of the race, I asked Father Dale Tornes to gather with the team. Father Dale was the pastor of Saint Stephen Catholic Church in Caldwell, which was the church Bev and I—along with most of the runners on the team—attended. We took a knee and Father Dale said a blessing asking God to help the team do the best they possibly could. That moment helped the runners get into the right mindset and put them at ease before the race ahead of us.

We hoped to go 1-2-3 in the state championship. To do that, we needed to neutralize Bill Seymour of Kirtland, which finished sixth overall in the Class AA division the prior season. With Kirtland moving down a division in 1986, Seymour was—like Caldwell—a decorated runner experienced against top competition.

Ahead of the race, I strategized and worked out a game plan centered around Tony.

Typically, Tony would gap people, put the hammer down, pull away, and finish first. But if he did that for this race, Seymour would probably finish second, and we wanted the three top spots. In order to go 1-2-3, we needed to tire out Seymour.

I envisioned Tony pulling him along and pouring the gas on, little by little, getting Seymour uncomfortable and into oxygen deficit, and *then* Tony could drop him like a bad habit. The farther he fell behind, the more it would give Brian and P.J. the chance to hunt him down and see how badly he wanted to kick for second or third.

---

20 "Ohio Cross Country Coaches Poll," *The Daily Jeffersonian* (Cambridge, OH), October 30, 1986.

OHIO HIGH SCHOOL BOYS AND GIRLS STATE CROSS COUNTRY MEETS

Scioto Downs
November 1, 1986

Julie Dias

Bob Henes

Richard L. Armstrong, Commissioner

Fred Dafler, Associate Commissioner

Blair C. Irvin, Assistant Commissioner

Clair Muscaro, Assistant Commissioner

Dolores A. Billhardt, Assistant Commissioner

Richard D. Termeer, Assistant Commissioner

Joanna Dias

OFFICIAL PROGRAM $1.50

SPONSORED & CONDUCTED BY
THE OHIO HIGH SCHOOL ATHLETIC ASSOCIATION

Cover — Pam Lewis

1986 Ohio State Meet Program

1986 Ohio State Meet Bib

IN TONY'S OWN WORDS I wasn't supposed to create a gap until the mile. I was supposed to string Seymour along with me and try to get him out to the 2-mile mark faster than he wanted to be. If he fatigued, it would give the others the best chance to out-kick him at the finish.

Tony immediately jumped into the lead, with Seymour alongside him. P.J. and Brian were close behind.

Seymour hung with Tony for the first half mile.

And the first mile.

About 1.5 miles into the race, Tony left Seymour in his dust. Seymour chugged along, falling behind but keeping Tony in his sights.

As Seymour fell further behind, a Caldwell runner raced ahead, but it wasn't P.J., who typically finished in second. It was Brian.

IN P.J.'S OWN WORDS When we got into that back field, when Brian went by me, he kind of tapped me on the backside and said, "Let's go." I didn't get into the kick with Brian and Seymour. But I was watching and cheering him on to beat Seymour in that last 200 meters. It was one of the few times ever I got to watch somebody else go at it, other than Tony.

Tony finished in 15:43. Just 10 seconds behind him in second place was Brian, who beat Seymour by a few seconds.

P.J. clocked in at fourth, followed by Stacy in eighth place and Randy in 11th. Our 1-2-4-8-11 finish gave the Caldwell team a score of 26. At the time, it was the lowest point total ever achieved at the state meet by any team, regardless of class.

Our top five runners finished before the first runner for second-place Convoy Crestview finished. Against *the entire team field*, we would have won with a 26–30 score.

1986 Ohio State Meet All-Ohioans
Caldwell Runners Tony (1), Brian (2), P.J. (5)

1986 Ohio State Meet Team Champions on podium

This was a total team victory—and a culmination of four years of dedication and commitment and success.

The final masterpiece.

The last meet of the greatest small-school cross country team ever assembled.

As we gathered at the podium, the crowd cheered and roared. Everything felt perfect.

This group had worked so, so hard and overcome every obstacle. The championship was a reflection of Tony's blazing speed and never cutting corners, P.J.'s vocal leadership and determination, Randy's heart, Brian's perseverance, Stacy's athleticism, Arnie's enthusiasm, and Danny's determination all coalescing to make us champions.

They had made a commitment to each other and to themselves to be their very best. And here they were, triumphant.

And yet, for Caldwell, it was all business on the podium—the ultimate display of sportsmanship. Our win the prior year was raucous. After so much heartbreak, we had struggled to contain our emotions that day.

The repeat title was marked by a different emotion—contentment. We were secure and confident. We knew we belonged there. It was an incredible feeling for a group of teens who'd faced so many challenges, not only difficult courses but also the tough terrain of poverty and broken homes.

The repeat champions posed together with satisfied smiles, and we as coaches were proud of their sportsmanship.

We achieved everything we set out to do. We didn't need to make a lot of noise. Our legs did the talking, and the results didn't lie.

IN RANDY'S OWN WORDS This was a veteran team. This was a team that had been to four state meets. This was a team that had moved up two years in a row to face the toughest competition. We had moved up during the season and had faced nine out of the 10 AAA teams who ran at state meet that day and we had beaten them all. We got to that starting line—it was four years for us, three for the younger guys—knowing what was expected and knowing what we needed to do.

The Cinderella story was complete ... or was it?

Coach Martin giving an interview

I thought we might be the best team in the country, and I wanted to prove it. Ego and pride played a role in that, but national recognition would also put Caldwell firmly on the cross country map. I wondered how we matched up against the Woodlands, the Texas team that had been ranked the nation's top team in preseason rankings in *Harrier* magazine.

It would have been interesting to have us meet in the middle, maybe somewhere around Memphis or Jackson, Tennessee, and run against each other.

Back then, there wasn't an easy way to know if we truly were national champions. Everything was so subjective. In my heart, I knew that we were the best, even if there wasn't some award or ranking to prove it.

Top Team rides fire truck in Welcome Home parade
Bottom 1986 Team: Front L To R Danny Lowe, Mark Rex, Brian Norris,
Arnie Ferguson, Dale Radcliff, Stacy Huffman, Brian Robinson,
Chris Fleming **Back L To R** Assistant Coach Dugan Hill,
P.J. Norris, Tony Carna, Randy Lowe, Head Coach Ron Martin

P.J. assisting Tony at Graduation, 1987

The team rose to meet every challenge. After we started racing against the bigger schools in 1985, we never lost again. Yes, you read that correctly. *We never lost again!* Our overall record for the 1985 and 1986 seasons was 273-0. You could find individual runners who were faster, like Bob Kennedy, but you couldn't find a team that could beat this team. Our guys had talent and put in the effort, but above all, they had heart.

I spent a lot of time soaking in the memories of 1986. I even brought out a video camera and captured some of the team's practices. I wanted to capture and hold onto those moments forever. Things would be different after that season. The runners at the heart of Caldwell's team—Tony, P.J., and Randy—were graduating. During their 4-year high school careers, their overall record was 535 wins and 2 losses. Those two losses came at state meets by a combined total of just 3 points. That's quite impressive, if you ask me. We had wanted to leave something lasting - a culture and a legacy. They did all that and were instrumental in starting a dynasty.

But the seniors weren't the only ones leaving. Things would be changing for me, too. I just didn't realize it at the time.

PART VI
LOOKING BACK

14.

MOVING ON

The mission was accomplished. We'd reached our goal. After Caldwell captured its second straight state title, I wondered what was next. The core of our team was about to graduate, and while the future was bright for the program, things would be different in the years ahead.

By now, I had been living, teaching, and coaching in Caldwell for 12 years. I'd learned a lot about training strategies, experimented with my runners to develop a scientifically based program, and worked with some amazing young men and their families.

Brrrrrrriiiiiiiinnng! Brrrrrrriiiiiiiinnng!

And then the phone rang. It was my high school coach, Norm Grimes from Tiffin Columbian High School. He was retiring.

"The job is yours if you want it," he said.

Did I want it? It was an enticing possibility. We had built something special at Caldwell. I could have stayed there forever. But there was something to be said about learning and growing and challenging myself to see if I could have the same success in turning around another program—and this was the high school I had attended as a student.

There were other factors beyond my own situation to think about, too. Our children, Chris and Heather, were getting older, and if Bev and I were going to make a move, we wanted to do it sooner rather than later, before they were of school age. Taking the Tiffin job would put us much closer to our parents and extended families. We didn't get to see them often enough since we lived more than three hours away. We'd always talked about moving back to northwest Ohio—but even so, the timing of the call was tough.

The pluses to taking the Tiffin job outweighed the minuses. But I needed to know that it was the right decision. So we sat at the kitchen table and I flipped a coin.

Heads we stay, tails we move.

I fished a coin out of my pocket and flipped it up, and time seemed to slow down as I watched the coin descend. Everything came down to this. Caldwell or Tiffin. Stay or go. The coin rattled against the table, *chh-chh-chh-chh-chh-chh*, and there was an American eagle staring at me.

Tails!

To be sure, we agreed to give it another toss, best two out of three.

Tails!

Okay, we said, one last time, best three out of five. Tails again. Bev and I sat and prayed hard about it, too. That was the most important thing.

Before making the final decision, I spoke with my assistant coach to ensure he would take over for me. I wanted peace of mind knowing the kids would be left in capable hands. He was the only person I trusted with the program. Luckily, he agreed.

The decision to leave Caldwell was not one I made lightly. I struggled with it. These were my boys, and I hated leaving them behind. However, I had to do what was best for my family. What made the decision an easier pill to swallow was knowing that the program was in good hands and that I would be leaving it in better shape than I found it.

I wanted to set that example for my runners, too. I always insisted that they leave camps, hotels, and cross country courses in better condition than they found them.

But even though I had peace of mind in my decision, that didn't make it any easier to discuss it with the athletes who made our success possible.

For the remaining runners like Brian, Danny, Stacy, and Arnie, I know things were difficult. I wasn't abandoning them, even if it felt that way. I wish I could have taken them all with me.

Even all these years later, it's still tough to learn how my departure impacted them.

IN BRIAN'S OWN WORDS I almost quit. It was three days after the track state meet, and I got the call from Ron, and he said he was leaving. It was like, *Okay, okay, okay.* Then after a few days, it just hit me. I was hurt and mad that my coach, who had been a guiding force for me over the last three years, was leaving me before my senior year. I thought for several days that I may just quit and go play football my senior year. Fortunately, my immaturity got a swift kick from my dad telling me there was no way I was giving up running. Even though the summer was tough without Ron, Danny and I really came together as seniors and focused on bringing the team together to keep the championship run going.

IN DANNY'S OWN WORDS We all were disappointed because we respect Ron and loved him. But we understood why he was moving on. He was going back home to his family. We thought he was going to coach us our senior year, and it was jarring when we found out he wasn't.

IN STACY'S OWN WORDS I can't say enough good things about Ron and Bev. I took a lot of things from those two. I was devastated when Ron left, and I lost interest in cross country after that.

Back then, even without the internet, word traveled fast. Caldwell was (and still is) a small town, after all. At the end of the school year, every teacher received a form with a simple question: "What are your intentions for the next school year?"

- Returning
- Not sure at this time
- No longer need employment

I normally checked the box next to "Returning." But not this time. I checked the box "No longer need employment," and I was on my way to my next adventure.

With my family in Tiffin and Bev's family nearby in New Riegel, we were perfectly set up to raise our kids near their relatives and in an outstanding school district. God opened the door, and the time was right.

I was excited to move back to Tiffin. But I also had a lump in my throat over leaving Caldwell.

After I announced I was leaving, the team made sure to get me back in a playful and endearing way. We had to make a trip to Tiffin to find housing, and I made the mistake of giving my assistant coach our house keys to keep an eye on the house. When we got back, the house and yard were covered in toilet paper. Even my family friend Sheriff Carl Runion, whose house we "decorated" during trips to Tiffin, never got it that bad. They even plastic-wrapped my toilet seat, which was an unpleasant surprise during my almost ritualistic homecoming "relief."

I called my assistant coach, and of course he played innocent. I also turned the prank around on him.

"Funny, now where did you guys put my TV set?!" I asked. He could see into my window from my front porch, so we moved the TV into another room where he couldn't see it, just in case he came up to look to see if my TV was truly taken.

Coach Martin's Tiffin house gets TP'd

Bev's dad (John Reiter) and Ron's sister (Bette Ann)
at the Tiffin Cross Country Carnival

"Honest, Ron, we didn't touch your TV!" he said.

"Well, it's gone, and if I don't get it back, I'll have to file a police report."

I let him stew for a few days before telling him the truth.

I didn't have a formal sendoff from Caldwell, which was just fine with me. The runners' parents graciously chipped in with $250 to help defray our moving costs, even though it wasn't something the families could really afford.

The guys came over to help us pack up the U-Haul, boxing up pictures and memories that would follow me forever. This was a true team, through and through, whether that involved cemetery runs or trophy presentations or taping up boxes.

The runners and their families had become family to us, and there was a bond between us that space and time could never diminish. Even after we left, a piece of my heart always remained in Caldwell.

When I arrived at Tiffin Columbian, a Class AAA school, I immediately recognized the challenge ahead. I would have to shift the team culture and tweak the training program.

Senior Danny Lowe

It was going to take some time and energy to spark a fire for this new group of kids similar to the one that blazed within the runners from Caldwell. It was an adjustment coming to practice and not seeing Tony racing in front and P.J. right behind him.

At the first practice, I asked the team, "What are your goals?"

They looked at each other and glanced at the ground before mumbling, "Well, we'd like to win the conference meet."

"Really?" I asked. "That's your goal? Your number one goal is to win the conference meet? What about the state meet?"

They all laughed. They had never reached the state meet before, and they didn't believe in themselves enough to think it was even a possibility. But as I told them stories about a little team from a small school across the state, they started to recognize the value in setting bigger goals.

"The thing that makes it so memorable is the confidence he had in what he wanted to accomplish with us," recalled Ron Combs, a senior member of the 1987 team. "I think that most of my teammates and I thought that Coach Martin was completely out of his mind when he listed our goals

Senior Danny Lowe

for the upcoming season. Our team had never threatened achieving such lofty goals. We had never been close to any of them, but there was something infectious in his confidence in what he wanted to accomplish and his belief that our team could do it."

It was actually a much easier transition than I expected. I took what I learned in my years coaching at Caldwell to my new job at Tiffin and promised the team success if they bought into the program. I was pleasantly surprised to see that they bought into the program very quickly.

We qualified for the state meet that first year—our dual meet record was 39–0, with an overall record of 611–102. In my six years at Tiffin, we won three district titles and we had four All-Ohioans in cross country, a team state runner-up, and one individual state champion (the late Alan Boos).

Meanwhile, I had left the Caldwell team in the familiar hands of my former assistant coach. I knew that the culture we created would continue through the efforts of Danny and Brian, who convinced Stacy to keep running with them in their senior year.

IN BRIAN'S OWN WORDS The team feel was much different. Stacy lost interest and we needed him, and Danny and I both knew he needed us. We leaned on our friendship more than anything, as we all became very close over the last three years. After much pushing, Stacy committed to his senior year, and while his heart wasn't in it as much as previous seasons, he was such a competitor, we knew it would happen on race day.

IN DANNY'S OWN WORDS Some of the runners could feel the culture of the team change and weren't showing up for morning practice. Most mornings we would stop by their houses and make sure they joined us. Brian and I were thrust into a different role after the three seniors and Ron left.

L To R Seniors Brian Norris and Danny Lowe,
Sophomore Arnie Ferguson, Senior Stacy Huffman

1987 Team Members L To R Stacy Huffman, Chris Fleming, Brian Norris, Arnie Ferguson, Danny Lowe, Mark Rex

I never stopped thinking of and supporting Brian, Danny, Stacy, and Arnie. And even though I had left, my heart was still with that team.

I would look for race results to see how they performed and got to see them at Tiffin and other meets—whenever I did, I always stopped and gave them words of encouragement.

It was frustrating to learn that the team stumbled and lost at Tiffin, their first loss in two and a half years. They were not running their best—but I knew they had greatness within them.

So I sent the runners a card.

I specifically called out Brian because I knew it would spark something in him and the team.

Well, I was right! The team started running like a team on a mission. They won every meet the rest of that season, including the state meet, where they scored just 25 points, setting a new state record for low team score and besting our 1986 score by one point.

Brian finished off his high school career with one of his greatest performances, winning the Class A race by a whopping 21 seconds.

With Tony and P.J. off to college, Brian was able to come into his own and become a star in his own right.

That 1987 team was also featured on ESPN's *Scholastic Sports America*, hosted by Chris Fowler. The sports network brought a camera crew to record Caldwell's team running at the Noble County Fairgrounds.

After the senior class graduated, Arnie stepped up to teach the next generation of Caldwell runners the lessons he'd learned from Brian, Danny, and Stacy. He became the glue and the anchor for a new era of Caldwell cross country runners.

1987 Team: Front L To R Bryan Clark, Danny Lowe, Stacy Huffman, Brian Norris, Paul Crum **Back L To R** Chris Fleming, Arnie Ferguson, Brian Robinson, Mark Rex, Head Coach Dugan Hill

The next generation of runners also saw some familiar faces during offseason training programs since some guys would come back and run with them during college breaks.

Caldwell's cross country program continued its winning streak for six more consecutive seasons, earning state championship titles from 1987 to 1992. That made eight consecutive state titles for the Caldwell High School cross country program, the most ever for any school of any division in Ohio history, boys or girls. Only a handful of schools in the country have ever won more consecutive state championships, and Caldwell—with nine state championships—is one of the most successful cross country teams in state history.[21]

Even after Caldwell became a cross country dynasty, it took some time for the team to get the proper recognition. And when it finally happened, it sure felt sweet.

---

21 Timothy L. Hudak, "Looking Back at the OHSAA's Cross Country Championships—Boys," OHSAA, https://www.ohsaa.org/sports/history/Tim_Hudak_Features/Cross_Country.htm.

15.
GREATNESS WINS OUT IN THE END

Everyone associated with Caldwell's 1986 cross country team—and even many of our opponents—knew that there was something special about our squad.

But at the time, it wasn't easy to get recognized nationally. Reporters at the *Harrier* magazine or the cross country publication MileSplit did their own research and comparisons before declaring a national champion, and you had to trust their analysis about teams they might not have seen in person or that hadn't raced against other top-ranked schools.

That started to change in 2004 with the launch of Nike Team Nationals, now Nike Cross Nationals (NXN), a meet held every November involving some of the country's top teams. Any high school can compete, and there are two races—seeded and unseeded. The winner of the seeded race is declared national cross country champion.

A national championship meet was not something we had the opportunity to experience in the 1980s.

In 2009, MileSplit was inspired to revisit national rankings for the years prior to the Nike Nationals and during the years from 1977 to 1989 when the *Harrier*—which revolutionized team national rankings in the 1970s—wasn't publishing end-of-season rankings.

A reporter reached out to Cincinnati Elder's coach, who suggested looking at Caldwell since we had beaten them at Tiffin and Malone that year.

When MileSplit published its 1986 national cross country rankings in August 2009, Caldwell was ranked number one. After all those years, we were recognized as national champions.

"No small school in the country has had as much of an impact on U.S. distance running as the Redskins from Caldwell," the article read. Caldwell "tore through the '86 season with a vengeance in an almost seek and destroy mentality."

The article also described the Ohio supermeet Tiffin Invitational and how I had moved the team up to the large school division: "It would seem no team had the answer for Caldwell."[22]

It was an unexpected honor, but one the team was deserving of.

We didn't seek out national recognition—at the time, everything we did was focused on winning the state meet. But it was both phenomenal and mind-blowing to be recognized on the national stage. It affirmed everything we felt inside about ourselves and this special team. It also felt good to be remembered.

> IN P.J.'S OWN WORDS It was really cool to look back and go, "Yeah, that was a freakin' special team, a special bunch of teammates and coaches." But that's kind of what it was. Because it was so far after the fact.

We'd gotten validation from the highest level of the cross country community. And in 2016, it was finally time to get recognition at Caldwell High School and celebrate our successes together. Three decades after our race with destiny, Caldwell honored all of its champion cross country teams. Ten banners were raised in the school's gym: nine banners celebrating the school's state-winning teams and one banner honoring the national champion team from 1986.

---

22 Aron Taylor, "XCLegacy: 1986 National XC Rankings," August 28, 2009, https://www.milesplit.com/articles/26334.

The ceremony took place between JV and varsity basketball games. It was a packed house. I don't think we'd ever had so many Caldwell runners in the same room together.

It was a monumental thing for Caldwell to be able to recognize so much winning. Most schools Caldwell's size might have one or two state championship teams, but nine? And a national championship on top of that? There was so much pride in the gym that night. There were smiles everywhere, a few tears of joy, and lots of hugs and high-fives.

National Championship Banner in Caldwell Gym

2016 L To R Head Coach Ron Martin, Arnie Ferguson, Danny Lowe, Randy Lowe, Stacy Huffman, Brian Norris, P.J. Norris, Tony Carna

IN P.J.'S OWN WORDS That night when the banners were unveiled, you could feel a lot of people appreciating what we accomplished. It was fun to share it with them.

IN RANDY'S OWN WORDS What really moved me was not only that the home stands but also the visiting stands stood up and clapped and acknowledged what we accomplished.

What made it extra special was that we were around to see it. The entire 1986 team made it back for this event, as did so many of the other championship squads. Some of us were a little rounder, with a little less hair (in my case, a lot less hair) than when we stood on the podium, victorious, all those years before. There were kids and grandkids and spouses and jobs to catch each other up on.

Even after so many years, the emotions and camaraderie between us were still just as strong.

As we watched the banners unveiled, it hammered home the team's resilience, grit, and determination. There were banners for the 1973 surprise team, the 1985 and 1986 powerhouse teams that never backed down from a challenge and slayed every Goliath in their path, and the continued dynasty from 1987 and 1992.

Set apart from a display honoring the state championship teams was a banner that was bigger than the rest, one that honored the 1986 national championship team.

As we stood together again, with the crowd applauding and shouting, our memories rushed back to the days where we ran our hearts out through farms, over roads, up hills and back down. We couldn't help but smile as we experienced our moment back in the sun.

To think we were once told we were too small to win! Proving that idea wrong—and showing others what's possible through teamwork—is the legacy these men will carry with them for the rest of their lives.

16.

BEING YOUR BEST IS A LIFELONG EFFORT

As I said from the very start of this book, this is not a story about Ron Martin. This is the story of an incredible group of young men who, despite facing challenging obstacles, came together to achieve incredible results.

Cross country served as a foundation for them to think big, strive for more, and achieve their very best. They've carried those lessons forward in major ways, becoming business executives and raising families and traveling the globe.

They've come a long way since their Caldwell days, when many of them faced money woes and personal struggles.

Here's what Caldwell's runners have achieved since their high school cross country days.

TONY CARNA

Tony attended the University of Michigan, where he was an eight-time letter winner and earned All–Big Ten and All-American honors. He helped Michigan to a sixth-place finish at the 1991 NCAA Cross Country Championships, finishing 21st overall (he was the 13th American finisher).

He graduated with a degree in kinesiology in 1992 and returned close to home to work at Southeastern Ohio Regional Medical Center in

Tony Then

Tony Now

Cambridge for the next five years. He spent the following 12 years in Columbus at Nationwide Children's Hospital. During that time, he also earned his MBA from Ashland University.

In 2010, Tony moved on to New York University Langone Medical Center to serve as the senior director of Sponsored Programs Administration and Research Enterprise Administrative Informatics, helping them navigate through Superstorm Sandy recovery and the doubling of their grant portfolio to $700M annually.

Tony now lives in Austin, Texas, with his wife Stacey and daughter Olivia, and serves as the assistant vice president for research and director of sponsored projects at The University of Texas at Austin.

IN TONY'S OWN WORDS Ron taught us that with a plan and hard work, we can achieve incredible things as individuals, but by appreciating the talents of our teammates and fully supporting them, we can accomplish amazing things together.

P.J. Then   P.J. Now

P.J. NORRIS

P.J. ran for Kent State University and earned varsity letters in both his freshman and sophomore years. But after his love of running waned, he flexed his leadership skills and explored other opportunities.

He became a founding father and president of his college fraternity (Sigma Phi Epsilon) as well as vice president of the Intramural and Campus Recreation Association. He pursued both law and business courses at Kent State and graduated with degrees in political science and business management.

After graduating in 1991, P.J. followed his father's footsteps and went into sales. He held leadership positions at Enterprise Holdings, AutoNation, and Autotrader (Cox Automotive). Today, he serves as the vice president of sales at Credit Acceptance Corp., where he has worked for the past 24 years.

IN P.J.'S OWN WORDS Ron didn't allow us not to be good students or good people. He taught us to be confident but not cocky. He built the strongest team culture I have ever been a part of, and my high school coaches were the best leaders I've ever had. My teammates were my best friends.

To this day, I still say that one of Coach Martin's strongest leadership points was that he never asked anything of us that he wasn't willing to do himself or hadn't already done. He led by example, as a coach and as a person. When you add to that the fact that our best runner (Tony) was also the hardest-working guy on the team, you really have the ingredients for success. While it was certainly a full team effort, Ron and Tony deserve so much of the credit.

RANDY LOWE

Randy chose Kent State University to continue his studies and keep running. He earned a varsity letter in men's cross country his sophomore year, but his cross country career ended after that year, as he needed to make money to stay in school.

He graduated in 1992 with a business degree with an emphasis in computer science. A lifelong learner, Randy also earned an executive MBA from the Ohio State University and spent time in China studying international business. He later earned a master's in cybersecurity and information assurance from Penn State University.

He spent his first few years in the workforce as a program analyst before becoming director of technology at the Longaberger Company, which sold baskets and lifestyle products, for 12 years. He's spent the last 17 years at American Electric Power, where he has served as a director of technology.

He married his high school sweetheart, Mindy, and they live in Caldwell with their youngest son, Camden. His family is extremely important to him, including his daughters Kailey, Rachel, and Paige; son-in-law Cory; grandsons Axton James, Tripp, and Boston; and son Tanner.

Randy has given back to his community by serving on the Caldwell volunteer fire department and as an EMT, along with serving as Special Deputy Sheriff of Noble County (OH), leading the Drone Task Force for Emergency Services leveraging drones like Search and Rescue. He is

Randy Then

Randy Now

an active member of St. Mary's Catholic Church in Fulda and serves on Caldwell's board of education.

Randy continues to run competitively and has completed five marathons, including the Boston Marathon in 2014. He also consistently participates in the Arnold Sports Festival's pump and run, where he performs the bench press and a 5K with his best friend, Brian Dimmering. In 2020, Randy finished third out of 661 competitors at the age of 51, and tied for the highest place for anyone over 50 years of age.

IN RANDY'S OWN WORDS Coach Martin instilled in me that when you have an opportunity, you can work hard and give it all you got, and the chips are going to lay where they are. If you work hard, I'm confident that you will be successful. I didn't compare myself to my teammates. I simply asked, "Did I improve myself? How much better did I make myself from my freshman year or even yesterday? Am I making myself better?" I take that mindset and I apply it to be a better husband, father, brother, Christian, and American.

Brian Then   Brian Now

BRIAN NORRIS

Brian received a full scholarship to run at Ohio University, but his collegiate cross country career had its ups and downs. He was injured as a freshman, but most of all, he missed the team culture and the small-town feel we had at Caldwell.

He came into his own as third man during his sophomore year, when the team was ranked 16th in the country. Ultimately, Brian decided to enjoy his college life a bit more and gave up running before the start of his junior year. He joined the Delta Tau Delta fraternity and focused on his studies in political science and criminal justice. One of his biggest disappointments was not seeing running all the way through—but his new direction helped him make connections and meet people that helped guide him in the years ahead.

After college, Brian worked in the public sector but realized it wasn't for him—he didn't want to just work toward a pension. His strong work ethic and friendship with Tom (Deuce) Ferguson, his former Caldwell cross country teammate, helped him secure a sales job at Kinkos (now FedEx). At Kinkos, he'd rise all the way to general manager.

He left that role to become vice president of sales at OfficeMax, and a year later was promoted to senior vice president of one of its business units. Brian left OfficeMax in 2008 and joined W.W. Grainger, where he was vice president of Services and Solutions for the $12 billion industrial supply company. Brian is now the president of Supply Technologies, a global supply chain management company based in Cleveland.

Brian resides in the Cleveland area and has been married to his wife Angi for 25 years. They have two children: Alyssa, who attends the University of Illinois, and Jake, a student at Virginia Tech. Brian rediscovered his love for running when his daughter started track and cross country in high school. She also went on to be a decorated runner in high school and earned a scholarship to run at Illinois.

IN BRIAN'S OWN WORDS There is so much I owe my teammates and my coaches from those incredible years. While I have been fortunate to have other mentors throughout my career, it was really Ron and my team who helped me build the foundation I needed to be successful in life.

He taught us how to lose with dignity and how to win with modesty. He taught us how to treat people with respect and take care of others when they may not be as fortunate, because that is what Ron did for us!

My teammates taught me about accountability and teamwork. A team that never wanted to let one another down, picked up the slack when someone wasn't at their best, and supported one another no matter how badly we did individually.

Those are the traits and lessons I am most proud of and that helped define who I am today.

Danny Then   Danny Now

DANNY LOWE

Danny joined his teammate P.J. and brother Randy at Kent State, but the team culture at college was different from Caldwell. Like his brother, Danny worked multiple jobs in college to make ends meet and put himself through school. He stopped running cross country after his freshman year.

Danny bounced around majors for a bit, dabbling in public relations and journalism before zeroing in on a dual major in real estate and business management. That pathway was the right one for Danny, as he went on to own and operate his own company, Lowe Real Estate Group in Caldwell. Prior to that, he worked for about two decades in the appraisal business for banks, attorney groups, and other large firms. Currently, he is a real estate broker specializing in flipping houses.

Danny got the itch for traveling when he competed at the Junior Olympics Track Athletic Congress, and to this day, he continues to travel, along with his son Aidan. Their goal is to visit all the state capitals in the United States.

IN DANNY'S OWN WORDS This was a special time in all our lives—to be a part of something greater than any one of us, and to do it with people you love as brothers. I wouldn't have traded that time for anything in this world.

STACY HUFFMAN

Stacy chose not to pursue college athletics—instead, he followed his artistic side, studying at the Art Institute of Pittsburgh and taking classes at the University of Pittsburgh and Carnegie Mellon.

He wound up getting a job with a relative at a trade company and working his way up to foreman. Stacy later entered line construction, building fiber optic and copper cables for communication networks, before becoming a network technician, which allowed him to work closer to home.

He's been married to his wife Erin since 2010, and they have been together since 2005. They live in McConnelsville, Ohio.

Stacy's passion is still art, and he does logo design and advertisements and is even trying his hand at woodworking.

Stacy Then

Stacy Now

IN STACY'S OWN WORDS Ron always stressed to us to go to class and show respect. I've held that near and dear to my heart throughout my life. P.J. and Brian's dad taught me to have a firm handshake and always look someone in the eye when you are talking to them. The advice and guidance have taken me a long way in life.

STEVE (ARNIE) FERGUSON

Arnie attended Malone College, one of the top running programs in the state of Ohio, and earned a varsity letter his freshman year, but he left after that semester because he didn't have the financial means to continue.

He transferred to Eastern Kentucky with some federal aid and financial support for his athletic involvement. He had a successful indoor season and made All-Conference in the 3,000-meter run. After being recruited to Ohio University, Arnie transferred for his sophomore season—he had to sit out a year so he didn't lose eligibility—and was later elected team captain.

Arnie Then

Arnie Now

Deuce Then

Deuce Now

In college, Arnie studied sports administration. A decade later, he earned his MBA from Ashland University. He followed in his brother's footsteps and worked at Kinko's in Missouri, managing a few stores and then entering their management training program. After about five years, Arnie went into chemical sales. He just celebrated 20 years at Henkel, where he serves as a director of Sales and Technical Service.

He's the proud father of Morgan, Maddi, and Nate.

> IN ARNIE'S OWN WORDS Cross country made me who I am today. It's given me the tools and opportunities to be successful outside of running. It also gave me an opportunity to see different parts of the country that I would never have had the opportunity to visit.

TOM (DEUCE) FERGUSON

Deuce graduated from Caldwell in 1985 and attended Ohio University, where he studied education. While in college he worked full-time at Kinko's, progressing from supervisor to assistant manager to manager at the young age of 22.

He continued to grow with Kinko's in leadership roles in Missouri, Texas, and Thousand Oaks, California, during his 16 years with the company. He was then recruited to Starbucks, which is where he's been for the past 18 years, holding many leadership roles across the globe, including his current position as president of the company's Latin America and Caribbean division.

He has had the support of his wife Becky for 30 years and two adult children, Mallory and Grant, who both also went to Ohio University. He currently lives in Columbus.

> IN DEUCE'S OWN WORDS The environment that Ron created instilled us with a strong work ethic, camaraderie, and loyalty, which I believe shaped who we are today. Looking back, I feel blessed to have grown up in Caldwell and been a part of the cross country program.

BRENT MARSHALL

Our senior leader of the 1983 team became a car salesman at a dealership in Charleston, West Virginia, and transferred his passion for running into a passion for golf.

Marshall fought two very serious battles with non-Hodgkin's lymphoma over the course of the past 12 years. His first encounter was a Stage 4 diagnosis, and it reared its ugly head yet again during the COVID-19 pandemic. While battling his second bout with cancer, Brent contracted COVID-19. He was given a 20 percent chance to beat covid and live without the assistance of a ventilator. I am happy to report that he is a survivor, and his cancer is currently in remission.

> IN MARSHALL'S OWN WORDS I don't know if I would have come through those things without what Ron taught us about mental fortitude and how to believe in yourself and the people around you. I still speak about being a cancer survivor at our cancer center here in Charleston,

Brent Marshall Then

Brent Marshall Now

> West Virginia, and I always bring up my coaches and talk about what they instilled in me. I don't know how I'll ever repay that.

BRENT SELLS

After graduating from Caldwell, Sells attended Muskingum College, where he met his wife Sharon, a fellow student. They married and eventually moved to Columbus, Ohio, where he had a chiropractic practice for 10 years before changing careers to join his wife in education. Sells started in the classroom as a chemistry teacher and is currently a high school administrator for Columbus City Schools.

He and Sharon have two sons: Blake, a graduate of Duke University who is currently a MD/PhD student at Washington University, and Samuel, a mechanical engineering student and college baseball player at Ohio Northern University. Sells has continued running over the years, having completed in more than a dozen marathons, including Boston twice.

Brent Sells Then   Brent Sells Now

IN SELLS'S OWN WORDS It has been said that all that
was required to be a successful runner was to "put one
foot in front of the other, faster each time." I took that
to mean that you should always focus on the present in
order to perform at your best. Running has been a constant
friend over the years during the good times and bad. It has
helped me stay rooted in the present. In nearly 40 years,
there hasn't been a single time that I've gone for a run
without thinking about Ron and the amazing athletes
that I ran with at Caldwell. The experience continues to
have an impact on my life, and I am blessed to have been
around such a quality group of people.

Ron Then   Ron Now

AS FOR ME ...

The lessons I learned at Caldwell translated into success at other stops in my coaching career, including Tiffin Columbian High School, Seneca East High School, Tiffin University, Heidelberg University, and Canal Winchester High School, where I coached until 2022.

I've "retired" multiple times throughout my career, but I just kept going back to it. It's just in my blood. I miss it. It's almost like a runner's high.

So now I stay involved by holding cross country camps every summer at Camp Pittenger, near Tiffin, Ohio; the camp where I met my wife Bev almost 50 years ago. I enjoy spending time with the runners and their coaches and sharing ideas.

Bev and I live in Canal Winchester, just southeast of Columbus and about 80 miles west of Caldwell. Living there allows us to be closer to most of our five children and eight grandchildren.

It's rewarding to see how the lessons I taught my cross country runners carried forward into their adult lives—and how far those lessons have taken them. For Caldwell's former runners, the pursuit of greatness provided a framework they've applied to every goal, challenge, and opportunity they faced.

17.
THERE IS SO MUCH CROSS COUNTRY CAN TEACH YOU

There is no other sport like cross country, and there is so much the sport can teach you.

My Caldwell runners have carried forward many life lessons from their cross country days. What they learned in high school cross country translated into the successful habits they carried into adulthood—both personally and professionally. Those lessons center around seven key themes:

- Family
- Hard Work
- Teamwork
- Confidence
- Perseverance
- Dedication
- Vision

FAMILY
Our cross country teams embodied family—we supported each other, challenged each other, and had each other's backs.

Bev and I nurtured that family theme by keeping our door open for the runners and by offering steady guidance.

I knew what it was like to grow up surrounded by divorce and hardship. For this group, the "team family" was everything, and at times they spent more time together than with their blood relatives. I aimed to be not just their coach but also like a father figure, just as my childhood and high school coaches had been to me.

> IN DEUCE'S OWN WORDS Many of us didn't have what I would call a traditional childhood. Whether it was single parents, money problems, or other life challenges, most of us had some sort of hole in our lives and cross country filled that gap.

HARD WORK

Running reinforced the work ethic these guys grew up with. They saw their parents working hard and trying to make ends meet. The value of their hard work was reflected by their results—those grueling 500 Mile Club days, hard work, and smart training were a recipe for success.

If you don't put in the effort, you cannot expect favorable results. While I think this group of young men was very talented, they'll tell you without question that they felt they were not the most talented team out there. So how do you beat talent? Hard work.

> IN DANNY'S OWN WORDS I know it's cliché, but hard work pays off. If we did not train the way we did, together, we never would have been as good as we were. If there's a goal I want to achieve today, I base my plan off of hard work first and then working smart about how I go about it. The work ethic I developed during my time at Caldwell has really set the tone for anything I choose to do.

TEAMWORK

These guys thrived off each other as brothers and friends. It wasn't just camaraderie; it was competition. They wanted to beat each other, and that made them stronger individually and as a group.

One of the cornerstones in putting together a solid cross country team is accountability. When the runners around you are all working hard, if you've built that solid team culture, they're not going to want to let each other down.

IN BRIAN'S OWN WORDS As a team, you learn to work together, you pick up where maybe your colleagues don't have strengths, and you positively influence one another … . But most important, you never want to let your team down. That is what an 18-year-old kid from a small, poor community learned many years ago, and it has been a driving force to me as a successful parent and businessperson.

IN DEUCE'S OWN WORDS There are three key things about building a great team, in my mind, and a lot of that comes from Ron and cross country. You've got to have a little fun, you have to care about your people, and then you need high expectations. If you just have high expectations without fun and caring about your people, your team will never move forward. Whether I'm leading a team in Japan or Latin America or in the United States, I've always focused on balancing those three things, and it's always resonated.

CONFIDENCE

Without confidence, it would have been impossible for us to succeed when we moved up to face larger schools. Caldwell's runners would have been intimidated.

Winning helped to build that confidence.

When you go through tough times, especially early in life, you might not start out with much confidence. However, as these kids developed a foundation, some scar tissue, and a support system around them, their confidence grew. And confidence helped to carry them far beyond their expectations and dreams.

IN P.J.'S OWN WORDS Whatever challenges I face, I tell myself, "I'm going to figure it out and figure out a way to win." I like being the underdog. That mentality has stuck with me my whole life, and it grew out of my time in Caldwell. I didn't have a lot of confidence at first in my running ability. But finding success helped me start to believe in myself. Working hard, following a process, and winning can change a person.

PERSEVERANCE

Giving up was not an option with this group. From Danny running through his back pain and dehydrating, yet continuing to put forth his best effort, to P.J. running with a swollen face after getting stung by a bee, these runners would not quit.

Even the heartbreak in the state championship meet reflected the runners' never-quit attitude. Caldwell's runners easily could have said, "The heck with it. We gave it our best shot and finished second in the state two years in a row." But they didn't. They persevered. They went back to the drawing board and came back with a vengeance.

They overcame so many obstacles that could have caused them to fail.

There are no guarantees. You can take the best team, put them out there, and still lose by two points. If something bad happens to a teammate, because of the weather or an injury, you still have to go out there and do your part and do it the right way. Never stop trying. Always push through to the finish line.

IN BRIAN'S OWN WORDS It wasn't until I was about 30 years old when I read the book *Good to Great* [by Jim Collins] that I realized what defined this team was the Stockdale Paradox. The Stockdale Paradox basically states, "You must never confuse faith that you will prevail in the end—which you can never afford to lose—with the discipline to confront the most brutal facts of your current reality, whatever they might be." We had lost the state meet twice. We came from a very small town, where we could barely field a team. We didn't have the same facilities and resources as the bigger schools. The cards were not in our favor. However, we overcame every obstacle and never stopped believing that we could be the best in the state.

DEDICATION

In running, perhaps more than any other sport, it truly matters what you do when nobody's watching. A basketball coach sees everything you do in practice on a contained court. But when you're running on the back roads, up in the farmland, no one is checking to see what you're doing. You could jog. You could loaf. You could cut corners. But if you want to be great, you have to dedicate yourself to it, because the next guy is waiting to pick you off and take your spot.

The runners' dedication was reflected in their commitment to offseason workouts—and their dedication brought results. The guys who participated in the 500 Mile Club saw some of the biggest improvements in their times.

The runners even had opportunities in the winter months to continue competing when I took them to out-of-town indoor track meets, and these offseason opportunities helped prepare them for the following track and cross country seasons.

Each of the runners made their own sacrifices and commitments to become better teammates. Danny gave up basketball and Stacy gave up wrestling, sports they both enjoyed, to run the winter 500 Mile Club.

Then there was Brian Norris running at the cemetery for practice when he was sick and absent from school. He showed up at the cemetery for practice, but I told him he couldn't practice if he missed school. So Brian ran the same interval workout as the other runners, but at a distance away from the team.

IN RANDY'S OWN WORDS Dedication to a goal often requires sacrifice, passing on short-term gratification to attain long-term success. When it is the pursuit of a team goal, you are sacrificing for your teammates.

VISION

Goals have to be tangible for there to be accountability every day. Each runner's goals were made public for a reason. It was to hold them accountable to what they said they were going to go out and do, but it was also to keep that vision fresh in their minds. From there, they could measure their progress, because if one guy said he was going to get out and place third but placed seventh instead, he knew he fell short. On the flipside, if someone wanted to be fifth and ended up third, that was a breakthrough. The point is that you can set goals all you want, but you have to know what steps you need to take to achieve them.

Then there's the vision of where you want to go next in life. High school is a pivotal time in a young person's journey. They have to decide what they want to do and where they want to be in the world. I am so proud that these guys were able to use cross country as a vehicle to go on and see and do great things in life.

IN BRIAN'S OWN WORDS Anything you do, you have to set a goal, but you have to understand how you're going to get there. You have to set these small building blocks in order to achieve that goal.

IN DEUCE'S OWN WORDS If there were any major lesson to be learned from Ron, it's that you have to work hard to be your best and to be a good person. The whole reason I studied teaching in college was Ron's influence. His mindset just works in life. Being from a small town of 2,000 people can be a disadvantage to anyone's growth and development, but Ron pushed us to think bigger than that!

I'm forever grateful for the chance to coach these guys. If it weren't for them, I wouldn't have had the opportunity to do the things that I've done in my lifetime. They're quick to give me credit, and I turn it right back around—they bought in and put in the work, and they deserve every good thing that comes their way.

CONCLUSION

I've always emphasized to my athletes how important it is to give back and share your knowledge with others. This book was borne out of that mindset.

I continue to give back to the sport I love by hosting cross country camps every summer for high school runners and their coaches. As my wife Bev says, you can take the coach out of coaching, but you can't take the coach out of the man.

I still get a kick out of watching kids' eyes light up when they accomplish something they never thought they were capable of accomplishing, interacting with parents, and continuing to learn and socialize with other coaches. Plus, you can't beat the thrill of the competition, the awards, the applause, and most of all, the fine moments of people cheering for those runners. There is so much positive energy at a cross country meet. There is nothing else in life quite like it.

I believe that God gave each of us a gift. And my ability to work with young people—and to help them achieve success in both running and in life—is one of my special gifts.

To learn more about our story and connect with us, visit our website, www.toosmalltowinbook.com.

It's been so special for me to recount the successes of the 1983–1986 Caldwell cross country teams. I hope the story and the lessons from those teams will resonate with you, just as they have with me.

ACKNOWLEDGEMENTS

Writing a book involves lots of support, and there are many people we wish to thank for their contributions.

We are immensely grateful to the runners from the 1983-1986 Caldwell Cross Country teams who contributed so much of their time, stories, and memories to help make this book a reality. We are honored to have been a part of this incredible story with them and we treasure the memories made during those remarkable years. Those team members include Tony Carna, P.J. Norris, Danny Lowe, Brian Norris, Stacy Huffman, Steve "Arnie" Ferguson, Brent Marshall, Tom "Deuce" Ferguson, and Brent Sells.

We're thankful for help from a number of writers and book experts, including Dan Good and Kevin Haslam, Tim Hudak, Kaylee "Kat"

2019 Ohio Legends XC Meet **Front:** P.J. Norris, Tony Carna, Randy Lowe, Ron Martin **Back:** Arnie Ferguson, Danny Lowe, Brian Norris, Stacy Huffman. **Photo Credit: Ted Rupe**

Tomsich, Roger Pickenpaugh, Isabella Talbott, Anna Perotti, Elissa Grasser, Julie Broad and the Book Launchers team, Marc Bloom, and XC Legacy research and reporting by Aron and David Taylor.

Local contributors included Marla Carr of the Noble County Historical Society, Lori Mitchell, Guernsey County Genealogy, Local History Clerk Red Edwards (RIP), and Cincy Elder Coach Steve Spencer.

Many people offered their reflections and helped to sharpen the book's stories, including Jack Hazen, JD Secrest, Matt Forshey, Dugan Hill, Herb Fitzer, Frank Fry, Matt Whitis, Jerry Fresenko, Ira Whentworth, Wayne Clark, Brent Lessuer, Ron Combs, Rick Sutak, Rob Sutak, Mile Split USA, Jordan Spence, Garret Stottsberry, Raegan Wheeldin, Blake Miller, Ethan Stritz, Jen Lorenz, Rebecca Herr, Diana Porter, Heidi Murrey, Charlotte Norris, Becky Ferguson and Jaimie Worstel.

Randy's family and friends provided lots of support: Mindy Lowe, Camden Lowe, Rachel Lowe, Kailey Lowe, Paige McGilton, Cory McGilton, Axton McGilton, Tripp McGilton, Boston McGilton, Tanner Harding, Larry and Jean Lowe, Randy Abrams (RIP), Jane Abrams, Duane Dimmering, Dennis Thompson and Maureen Dimmerling.

Special thanks also goes to Ward and Shirley Murrey, Ward Murrey, Jr., and Delores and the late Paul Jonard.

Ron is very thankful for the family and friends who encouraged him to bring this story forward and for family members who spent hours helping with the book. There are numerous other people he wishes to thank, especially the runners who brought his coaching career, and his life, so much meaning.

During his 12 years of coaching cross country at Caldwell High School from 1975 through the fall of 1986, this includes: Brian Jonard, Bill Jonard, Jack Cox, Donny Snodgrass, Dale Snodgrass, Brad Radcliff, Dave Hanes, Steve Warner, Dave Fleming, Bryan Anderson, Dean Capello, Doug Hayes, Allen Miller, Van Colley, Marty Jennings, Sam Schoeppner, Tim Hayes, Dannie Wilson, Mark Kovach, Glen Harper, Craig Ferguson, Doug McLaughlin, John Powell, Glen Haga, Randy "Poke" Ferguson, Scott Miller, Mike Bruggeman, Doug Buckey,

Scott King, Brent Marshall, Tom "Deuce" Ferguson, Mike White, Bill Singer, Jerry Ditch, Brad Braden, Kelly Saling, Todd Schell, Lori Schoeppner, Renee McFarland, Kim Singer, Melanie Morland, Kristi Morland, Holly Zimmer, Andrea Moore, Jane Walters, Sherry Bever, Tony Carna, P.J. Norris, Randy Lowe, Brent Sells, Brian Norris, Danny Lowe, Stacy Huffman, Chris Fleming, JD Secrest, John Garrett, Steve "Arnie" Ferguson, Brian Robinson, Mark Rex, Dale Radcliff, Annette Nau, Beth Radcliff, Barb Lowe, Kelly Walters, Renee Nau, and Shannon Koval.

Thanks to the early Caldwell Cross Country Teams (1971-1974) and their coaches for building the foundation for a successful program before he arrived. Hats off to the 1971 Inaugural Team and the 1973 State Championship Team! Congratulations to the 1987-92 teams for their state championship titles and thanks for keeping the streak alive!

Mentors, coaches, and friends who inspired Ron on his journey include Coach Norm Grimes, the Late Coach Milt Place, Coach Dugan Hill, Coach Rod O'Donnell, Sebastian and Peter Coe, Coach Jeff Phillips, hundreds of coaches and athletes from Team Camp of Champs, and all of his runners from Caldwell, Tiffin Columbian, Seneca East, and Canal Winchester high schools, Tiffin University and Heidelberg University, as well as the runners' parents and supporters.

Special recognition goes to Coach Jack Hazen and Coach Joe Vigil who influenced Ron the most and helped him develop into the coach he is today. A very heartfelt thank you for their continued friendship.

Most of all, Ron wishes to thank his wife Bev and their family: Chris Martin, Heather (Martin) Faerber, Erica (Byers) Martin, Rachel Martin, Rebecca (Martin) Bair, Kristin Martin (Chris's wife), Kyle Faerber (Heather's husband), Kris Byers (Erica's husband), Andrew Bair (Rebecca's husband), David Knight (Rachel's fiancé), and grandchildren Blake, Brady, Aubrey and Cooper Martin, Reiter and Renner Faerber, and Briggs and Monroe Byers.

www.ingramcontent.com/pod-product-compliance
Lightning Source LLC
Chambersburg PA
CBHW071733120626
46550CB00002B/510